13

Miracles *in* Montanare

TEN YEARS IN TUSCANY

BY

LARRY SNYDER

Photography by Larry Snyder

IRONTWINE
—PRESS—

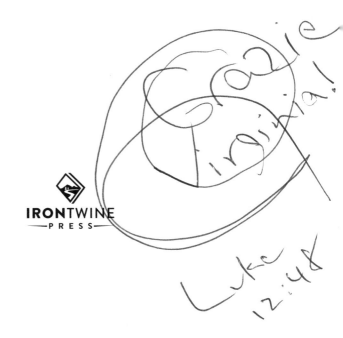

Grazie
Virginia!

Luke
12:48

For Jill, Daniela, and Momma Jean.

Miracles *in* Montanare: TEN YEARS IN TUSCANY
www.TenYearsinTuscany.com

Published by Iron Twine Press
www.irontwinepress.com

Photography by Larry Snyder / Fotoitaliana - Images of Italy
www.TenYearsinTuscany.com

Book design by Sonja L. Gerard

Front cover photo: San Galgano, Italy
Back cover and Chapter *The Dirt Road (2004)* photo: Piazzano, Italy

Printed in the United States of America.
Paperbound edition of this book originally printed by:
DCG One, 4401 East Marginal Way S, Seattle, WA 98134
www.dcgone.com

ISBN 978-0-9970600-0-3 (pb)

10 9 8 7 6 5 4 3 2 1

— Contents —

Preface

Forty years ago, my grandfather told me above anything else in life, including wealth, fame or status in the community, the most important things you'll ever treasure are your friendships. Little did I know at the time, on the other side of the earth awaited a group of friendships, a human experience, that has created most of who I am today and most likely will always be.

The title of this work is no casual choice. ***Miracles in Montanare: Ten Years in Tuscany*** recounts a decade of learned lessons in love, vulnerability, and passion. Without a shared language, similar family traditions, or understanding of cultural norms, Jill and I took a chance. It paid off in ways no one, including ourselves, would ever have thought possible. This is a small collection of our favorite stories and although they don't follow a typical timeline, my hope is each one will provide a window into our unique experiences living on foreign soil.

This is our story. I hope it engages your imagination and fires a desire to make a similar plan. Living outside the confines of our comfortable, digitally-connected, over-committed American life is not only refreshing but it might save your life. Francesca, Primo, Piero, Luisa, Amedeo, Rosy—the caring Italians who became our dear friends and whom you will meet in this book—took us all the way into their world. We've attended their weddings, birthdays, and even cried together when our community of 150 lost a family member. Italians by nature are a loving, open, and very compassionate people, but even they have boundaries normally reserved for blood kin. The experience you're about to jump inside is rare. Even Italians, or those who have lived amongst them for decades, are bewildered by why an Italian village on the Tuscan/

Umbrian border would embrace an American family at such a deep level. Part of the answer is our 10-year-old daughter, Daniela. As you'll discover, she is our miracle.

If you don't believe in miraculous events, this story is not for you. Almost everything that occurs in Montanare falls into that category. If you are open to how feelings are more important than words, gestures outweigh plans, and traditions are honored almost like muscle memory, **_Miracles in Montanare: Ten Years in Tuscany_** as a book might have the same life-altering effect the experience had on us.

Firenze

Starting at Rock Bottom
2002

I've been on two blind dates in my life. The first was an ill-conceived arrangement by my oldest sister when I was 14. The last is the one I'm still on, a dozen years after it began.

One night in December 2003, at The Rock Bottom, an upscale brewery bar in Bellevue, WA, with dozens of people unknown to me, I joined the birthday celebration of a woman I'd come to meet for the first time. As I hit the last of the two dozen stairs to the upper level of the noisy bar, my brain took notice of what I was getting myself into. Seated at a long bar-height table, 12 sets of eyes greeted my entrance. This felt like a contemporary episode of *The Dating Game*. Being on that late 70's show was never my dream. I worked my way around the table trying not to give away my elevated pulse. Conveniently, the only open chair was next to a well-dressed blond gal sporting a black and white skirt. I extended my moist right hand and took up my pre-arranged parking spot. My knowledge coming into this adventure was limited. I knew only that her name was Jill and that, because we shared an affinity for all things Italian, friends decided the idea of our meeting had merit. My admiration for Italia was ignited after a college study abroad to Rome and Jill's took hold after she joined a small tour company's inaugural circuit of the old country. As a youngster I was content to leap and then look; "Hey, watch this!" was my best line. But matters of the heart in mid-life require a bit more caution.

Last call found my new friend Jill and me alone, all others bound for home. This conversation was far from over. A dinner was planned. Italian would be on the menu. The guest list would include a tight selection of the best from this birthday bash. If the first date was my audition, the forthcoming dining room appearance would be my official dress rehearsal. Monitoring my logic, I began asking myself some serious questions. Is cooking an authentic Tuscan meal for ten a good debut? Perhaps a good selection of prosecco, reds, whites, and limoncellos would numb palettes enough to give the meal a pass and provide me a chance to stay in the game.

Creating a culinary experience together when you have little or no past can really only go one way or the other. The little past we did share, beyond our marathon first conversation, was a mutual admiration for the first cookbook of Italian chef and resident of Tuscany Roberto Russo. His recipes gave us a roadmap for success in the kitchen. After all, it was this Napolitano transplant to the Tuscan/Umbrian border that brought us together. Chef Russo's beautiful Parco Fiorito, the 16th-century convent-turned-Tuscan-Farm-Stay, was our common thread. Jill and I had both stayed there. Our travels to Parco Fiorito didn't land in the same year but those we traveled with were of the same blood. For one night, then, our goal would be to join our paths, to combine our efforts and deliver to our friends the tastes that conjured the place we both dreamed of being.

The premier of *Cucina* Jill-and-Larry was a smash hit. A line of spent wine bottles along the kitchen rail proved it to be true. The reviews came back positive. Our mission to recreate the flavors, sounds, and energy of Chef Roberto in a kitchen 5,000 miles from their origin felt genuine according to the hostess and her dozen invitees. Without question, it was this well-dressed and cultured Italian man that demonstrated the elements of a nation by which I am now intoxicated. With nothing but crumbs from the flourless chocolate decadence littering the table, our staff of evaluators headed for the exits and Jill and I found ourselves in a stare with a little more history. This is when the real dance began. Having grown up with five sisters, I knew what pulling petals meant…*she loves me, she loves me not, she loves me.*

Comé No?

All four stacks of documents on the kitchen table (that was now ours together) grew with each passing day and spoke volumes about where those petals had landed. To move to Italy for a year, we knew we would have to appear before the Italian Consulate in San Francisco and make our case for a visa. Jill labored to make our file of documentation all-encompassing and beyond reproach. For at least a month, our evening activity involved tracking down everything from notarized birth certificates for me and Jill to financial statements that documented what we hoped would be the appropriate balance to make the grade. We had been told that to be granted one year residence in Italy one must prove financial status adequate to cover the expenses of the year. When we pressed for more information—*what is an adequate amount to cover a year's expenses*—the response was classically Italian: *Enough to cover what you are likely to spend.* The ambiguity of Italy's government documents was beginning to shine light on our different personalities. My sense was that this impending trip two hours south would be yet another opportunity to use my DNA-embedded persuasion skill set. Jill, on the other hand, wanted her color-coded three ring binder—collated in the exact order as described on the Italian Immigration website—to do the talking. If opposites attract, Jill and I are a perfect match.

Although my travels have taken me between Seattle and San Francisco on countless missions, never has a flight had so much opportunity riding on it. With little, if any, carry-on luggage and absolutely nothing with our names on it in the cargo hold, Jill and I shared a high-anticipation sigh as we went wheels up. After months of Jill's diligent research, our request to have an audience with the Italian Consulate was about to be granted.

In her Gucci-cut navy suit and well-chosen Ferragamos, Alessandra rapidly thumbed through Jill's carefully assembled documents noting the certificate of health care coverage and suitable financial information. We both noted the lack of conversation, odd for a meeting with an Italian, thinking there might be a bit of Q&A at some point. Exactly 90 seconds into our California get-together, Alessandra set her green, designer glasses on the antique desk and said, "Va bene."

Even with my limited handle of Dante's lingua pura, I get the translation for very good or OK in Italiano. Jill was looking for a more definitive version of va bene and asked the government official: "Does that mean we get to go to Italy for a year?"

Pushing her chair back and standing as if to say *this gathering has reached its conclusion*, the brunette looked at us with hands open and quipped, "Comé no?"

Waiting till the large wood security door completely closed, I wrapped Jill in my arms and we both let out a muffled yell. The reluctance I read in Jill's aquamarine eyes led me to worry her mind was saying this year-abroad-endeavor was a poor idea. Her reservation, though, was purely a pause borne of linguistic interpretation: If va bene gave her caution, comé no (why not) was hardly a shiny, unequivocal, capital YES!

Seventy-two hours later, I gratefully signed for an official document while sipping my morning Americano. The sole contents: two blue American passports. Securely occupying an entire page in the middle of each: a most beautiful green *Residenz Elettiva Visto* hologram. Knowing this breaking news would create a game-changing detour in Jill's accomplished software career, I hesitated making the call to her office.

And Then There Were Three

Just twenty-four hours before her early December debut, the speaker phone blares in our Seattle living room. Amedeo and Rosy quickly recall a rate we can handle. Although they prefer Ferrari-speed conversation, ours is more like a Sunday stroll. Without the presence of flailing hands, drawings in the sky, and expressive facial gestures, we silently acknowledge our foreign tongue is getting worse by the week. Jill and I try to explain our degree of thanks for the four-piece pink knit outfit Rosy must have spent months creating by hand.

"Molto grazie, molto grazie. Questa regalo come non altre (This gift is like no other, thank you very much)." My glazed-over chestnut eyes make it obvious to Jill that my Italian words are running thin.

Although this distant phone exchange is important, Jill's immediate mission is managing and documenting the strength and intensity of contractions. Following multiple *ciaos* and *arrivedercis*, we finally click the cordless handset off. Once again, we realize our hearts live in three places. Although we travel with the familiar blue American passport, a portion of our soul now lives up a dirt road in the tiny eastern Tuscan village of Montanare. The rest of our spirit is split between my birthplace, Seattle, and Jill's native western Michigan.

"Three minutes and really strong," Jill notes. I keep trying to recall what our birthing classes advised for the magic time to pack the car. Having moved just a dozen days earlier, the chances of my finding the sacred class notes is remote but the number three does ring a bell.

A call to the OB proves, like most other Daniela-preparation steps, to be laughable. "You will know," the calm nurse assures us. "Once you can't walk or talk, it's time to come in."

Although I want to grin and chuckle, a concerned Charlie Brown smile seems more appropriate. Back in Kalamazoo, Michigan, a rookie grandma awaits the news. Jackie has waited four decades for her daughter to add the next generation. My mom and dad sit in the waiting room. In Italy, all proclaim Daniela will be an Italian by association. Amedeo and several *amici Italiani* have made it clear that our year in Italy eating their country's best food, finest extra virgin olive oil, and, of course, sampling plenty of Italy's best wine, are the reasons for Daniela's European conception. There is little in these assertions I find hard to believe. We did, after all, grow most of our own food, cook with the world's best olive oil and enjoy plenty of wines we couldn't possibly afford back home. The combination of a freezing Tuscan gale, our final liter of Chianti Riserva, and one week left in paradise had made the scene perfectly fertile.

Little time passed before everyone half a world away knew of Daniela's arrival. Our gregarious Italian friend, Chef Roberto Russo, took the e-mail news to most of Tuscany and Umbria. Upon arrival home with Daniela, the voicemails rang out—

Evviva-Daniela Arriva! It took us a week to figure out Hurrah! has an Italian equivalent.

Daniela has Jill's aquamarine eyes. Her lips and nose resemble what I see each morning in the bathroom mirror. She is our own miracle made from a series of miracles: that Jill and I found each other on that first blind date; that Italy held such a strong place in our separate hearts that it instantly became the thread that knitted them together; of a conception when we felt aged out of that opportunity; and the unlikely community of friends and family we forged out of a group of strangers half the planet away from our home. Daniela is our miracle who reminds us of the miracle of the life we have been blessed to live more than ten years in Tuscany.

Panzano in Chianti

Friendship is a Place
☙ 2014 ☙

Friendship can be measured many ways. Some friendships stand the test of time, some a distance half a world away. As our Delta 330 pushes east through several times zones, a dozen thoughts run through my head and heart. This journey marks one decade of Tuscan summers in our beloved Montanare. Our native friends ask us *Why Italy* when they see the large suitcases near the door, as if to say, *Why not visit another part of the world?* Other friends have made the European trek with us and know the answer, wishing they could return soon.

I've lost count of the number of times the question *Why Italy* has come my way.

I have a feeling most of us led the life of an Italian in a previous existence. It could be I've had several and I'm now revisiting them. Even after more than a dozen trips, my energy still elevates when the wheels touch the Fiumicino runway, 45 minutes outside of Roma.

Italy is life unplugged for me.

Italy is free of limitations on the expression of love, energy, and, most of all, passion. Greeting close male friends with a peck on each cheek is natural. Waving my hands to match the emotion

I'm trying to express comes without thought. Being free to move in sync with the music is the norm.

Few things, though, are equal to the nonverbal play around the dinner table.

Leaving the confines of our comfortable American life isn't difficult, knowing a village of friends and a completely different human experience awaits us. Those cultural priorities on American soil, including wealth or position in society, are not relevant in our Italian life. It's much more about eye contact, the moments before us, and a new definition of personal space. I now look forward to my dear friend Ame gently resting his hand on my forearm speaking at an unnecessary volume while I enjoy the aroma of his cigarette breath.

Once the forward cabin door opens we begin looking for familiar sights. Even in Italy, the land where nothing ever really changes, we notice a shiny new concourse has appeared. The well-suited Italians, each with mobile phone against ear, use their free hands to accentuate their conversations. The scent of fine cologne and perfume fills the air, a constant in most public places that suits me well. In a well-traveled Ziploc sandwich bag remain the Euro coins from our previous trips.

We've arrived with much more than four adult arms can manage so an Italian luggage cart is in order. I ask Daniela to look around and perhaps we can save our two Euro coin by spotting an abandoned cart. No luck.

In addition to the Roman Forum, another place where time stands still is the airport car-rental office. With 12 customers holding numbers, two very relaxed agents serve the sleepy transatlantic arrivals. Although I shouldn't, I always introduce little Daniela first to provide a bit of personal connection. It often results in a magic upgrade; this trip is no exception. Behind the counter, Alessandro asks a familiar question about the origin of Daniela's very Italian name. After I explain that we named our daughter after the administrator of our Umbrian sister city office, another premium appears: Alessandro passes keys to a new Audi instead of a Ford.

At four lanes wide, the well-maintained *strada* leaving Leonardo da Vinci Airport is a first opportunity to renew my passion behind the wheel. U.S. driving laws under-actualize one's ability to use adrenaline and momentum as a driving strategy. When asked about driving in Italy, my response at home is always the same. The speed limit is easy to remember: it's as fast as the fastest car can go. If you cannot be that, move over immediately or welcome the car behind you into your trunk. Even the Italians recognize my affinity for the left lane, although it's become dinner table discussion on a too-regular basis.

Without reason, and only for tradition, the over-freeway Auto Grill just outside Rome captures us one more time. A clean bathroom, the first of many *doppio* espressos, a useless toy, and one barely-cold Coca Cola Lite give us what we need to make our six speed roll north. Once free of Rome early-evening traffic, our well-powered euro car gets happy and our three-hour trek becomes two and change. We each shout out familiar spots including La Tufa, our most favorite Pizzeria in Ossaia, the packed bar in Pergo, and the rectangular black and white sign announcing our destination, Montanare.

At a slight rise, the one-lane, unimproved road passes the beautiful gated Medici-style 16th-century villa of Alfanso and Agnese, the painter Giuliano's house on the left, and with one last turn we spot Primo and Francesca's Tuscan-yellow two story compound.

It's at this spot our language worries set in. We're about to enter a world without one word of English. Though we speak Dante's lingua pura just a few weeks a year, with few exceptions, I've never been afraid to use the 100 (or so) Italian words I know by heart. They're not in the right order and often well outside of the proper context. My 100 words, my creative combinations of them—along with my earnest pantomimes—have grown into their own pidgin language, officially deemed, by our endlessly bemused Italian friends, Larriano.

This unique adaptation of a foreign tongue has proven useful on a daily basis including when the subject matter is technical. As when, during our first year at Montanare, Jill and I needed to stay robustly connected to the internet. I attempted to ask neighbor Maurizio about the possibility of a Wi-Fi signal worthy of our U.S. security standards. I took a stab at it in Larriano Italian: "Please add a giant muscle on your chimney with a signal strong enough so we can make money on our PC." Maurizio's response the next morning: "Non ć è problema!"

Jill, on the other hand, wants to demonstrate her respect and desires to speak in the fashion the language was designed. That's a tall order and those who love us find Larriano a passable method of sharing thoughts and feelings with me, using the limited number of words I know. Somehow we never struggle to understand each other.

The gravel under tires alerts residents of our approach. The wide spot in our rural passage is between Primo's house and Cà di Maestro's giant iron gate.

With anticipation and collective nerves, we slowly back the Audi between Cà di Maestro and the Casina, home to owners, Piero and Luisa, for 120 days a year. Before the car has come to a rest Rosy has rushed to meet us and is opening the passenger door. As is tradition, Daniela is lifted from the back seat and Jill and I are embraced, all as if to say, *wherever you have been, you are now back where you belong.*

That is why Italy.

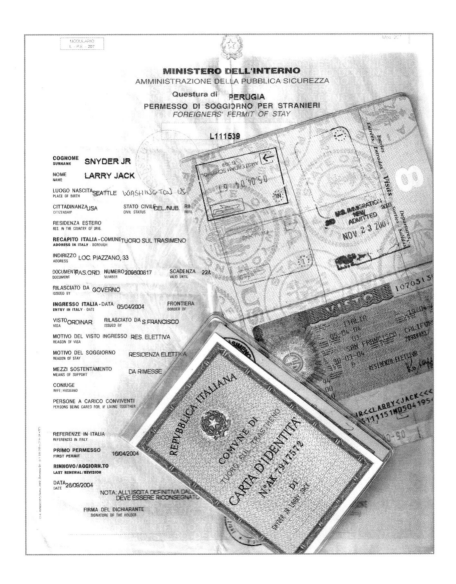

Can't leave home without it.
Documentation to enter and stay within Italy.

Siena

Italians by Association
2003

I've always had a hard time saying no when I believe a good time or a good reason is attached to a proposition before me. Chef Roberto Russo must have known this before he called.

"Francesco is coming to Seattle," he declares.

I'm not quite sure who Francesco is so I keep listening. Roberto now fills in the important blanks. Francesco is Vittorio Accioli's 23-year-old son. Roberto and Vittorio have partnered on property development projects, among other endeavors. The Tuscan-born, designer-outfitted Vittorio has built a small local business empire to include a very active insurance agency, an accounting firm, and a couple businesses the function of which I've yet to determine. He's assisted the formation of the local soccer club, and has his name on three boutique hotels. Vittorio has created his own La Dolce Vita and he's determined his two sons will follow suit.

Francesco is trying to follow in the footsteps of his all-accomplished older brother, Alessandro. The younger appears to have taken collateral damage from his parents' split when he was just three. His love of office work is half that of his senior brother. Tama, as Francesco is known to his friends, would rather create a memorable five course meal with exact wine pairings than push paper around a desk. His mission in my hometown is to earn an English Language Learner certificate.

"He needs to speak English and will attend a three month college course near your house," Roberto tells me.

Roberto failed to notice the 30 mile trek through the middle of downtown Seattle required to reach Shoreline College from my house. Having Tama stay with me would not be a practical option. Happy to help, nonetheless, I conveyed to Roberto I would have to put some time into finding a convenient place for the soon-to-be-student to live.

"He will arrive in four days," the Chef responded. It seems that alerting me that I had unilaterally been appointed responsible for Francesco's lodging and keep while in Seattle was last, not first, on Roberto's list.

Still, I believe great things can happen when you say yes. Even when you don't know exactly how you'll succeed, if you keep faith in yourself and those around you, saying yes can lead to magic.

I engaged my creative thinking and remembered Elbie, a special friend and former colleague who lived very near to Francesco's future classroom. It was tough for me to give her a raving endorsement of the young Cortonese, except to say rent would be paid on the first and she'd never be disappointed if he was making dinner. Elbie was open to the idea and in 48 hours prepared to take in a young man neither of us had ever seen or met.

After a mad rush of cosmetic improvement projects to my new best friend's north Seattle home, my next task was collecting this stranger from SEA-TAC Airport.

When the human rush to collect baggage had cleared, a travel-worn young man in orange pants sat patiently waiting. Using the very early form of Larriano—my self-styled, pidgin Italian—I welcomed Francesco and we motored north.

Our journey included finding common words which would become our conversation. We recycled *grande, bella,* and *tanti* 50 times in 30 minutes when trying to express that things in Seattle appear big, beautiful, and plentiful. Francesco hadn't seen a building beyond 10 stories in his two decades of life. In Italy, with very few exceptions, a building cannot exceed the height of the *Duomo,* or tallest church. He'd also not experienced a road that stretched five lanes wide, as even highways in Italy are just a pair of lanes in each direction.

I did my best to explain all I knew about Francesco's host family, including the important fact that English was the official tongue and not to expect even the slightest bit of Italian to start. Our arrival was comical and it was at this point that I began seeing what a crazy position I'd put Elbie and daughter, Morgan, into. After a brief tour and a few moments to get settled, Tama took a chair in the TV room. His first experience with American TV couldn't have been more unusual. Johnny Knoxville, Steve-O, and Bam had just released *Jackass: The Movie* to DVD and 15-year-old Morgan's infectious laugh had Francesco going in mere moments. No longer in my Secretary of State welcoming hat, I decided these two would make things work just fine and Tama's first English slang would most likely be a set of spicy words from this R-rated madness.

Forty-eight hours later, Jill and I made the trek across town to visit Francesco. When we arrived he was nowhere to be found. Not having a house key, I called, knocked, yelled and even tried every window. I'd yet to give him my extra mobile phone so I had no way to ring him and I was sure he wouldn't respond to the home phone. Trying to avoid panic, we withdrew and sat over lunch wondering how many years it would take for Francesco's family and friends to forgive us for losing one of their own.

Returning to the house an hour or so later we noticed the front door ajar and Francesco inside the house. Trying not to act too motherly, Jill did her best to explain we'd been looking for him. I took notice of three grocery bags on the kitchen counter, one from DeLaurenti's, a well-known, family-owned Italian shop at Seattle's Pike Place Market. In less than two days, Francesco had figured out the Metro bus system and made his way to downtown Seattle. He'd done plenty of research prior to this voyage to the new world, including where to buy authentic meats, cheeses, spices, and wines to do his part in the kitchen. That night, Francesco made good on the narrow list of benefits I had used in my sales pitch to Elbie. Eight of us raised our wine stems while apron-clad Tama shared the culinary passion instilled by his mom, Fiorella, and Grandmother Anita.

The next night found Francesco in more unknown territory. His early-spring arrival coincided with the ramp up of my fundraising auction season. Seated at a round table with Jill and eight others, the young Italian watched with utter confusion as patrons' arms went up and down, donating to a local symphony orchestra. An attendee at the adjacent table recognized Jill's attempt to translate some basic table top items like fork, spoon and knife. Composer Donald Stewart wrote his full symphony in Siena, just an hour from Francesco's birthplace. He slid his chair near and took on Jill's dual language task. For the first time in three days, there was a collective sigh for all. The young composer became an immediate local resource for all things Italiano. His mobile number was added to my contacts. Donald too, eventually benefitted from Francesco's fabulous work in the kitchen.

The word eventually got out that an Italian chef was cooking four nights a week. Elbie's home was rarely without a heavy, mouthwatering aroma. Francesco became the very best customer of Central Market and was often pulled aside to share his menu for that evening. The deli knew how he liked his prosciutto sliced and wrapped. The meat cutter was well acquainted with how Tama needed his steaks trimmed. Even the bakery saved pugliese bread so Francesco could craft his delicious *bruschetta* and *crostini*. As a beneficiary of this culinary nirvana, I began to realize it was not the dry cleaners shrinking my slacks. This incredible feast of flavors several days a week was starting to tip my bathroom scale. The combination of crème added to the pasta sauce, heavy helpings of rosemary-and-fennel roasted potatoes, oversized portions of tiramisu, all washed down by Tuscany's best vino rosso was making me grow. Being just one month into this, I began imagining what I would see in the mirror after my full 90 days with Francesco. Elbie was also feeling the effect while getting dressed in the morning. This Italian restaurant in her house did a number on her sleep pattern too. It was decided that Cucina Francesco was to be open for Sunday dinner only.

Each week the table grew in length to the point where extra chairs accompanied arriving guests. As his English class neared its finish, Tama was speaking fluent English. His father's desire of having a staff member able to read and respond to EU documents was about to be realized. Francesco wasn't looking forward to that part of this adventure. We dreamt of opening *Caffe Fiorella* in downtown Seattle, dedicated to his beautiful mother.

Our final dinner together required most of the living room furniture to find another home. Two dozen of us raised our glasses at least that many times to share our appreciation for the chef who had added to our waistlines, increased our cholesterol, and allowed us to be Italians by association for three months.

Since that experience with Francesco, I have enjoyed years visiting him in Italy with Jill and Daniela. Our experiences have shown me that the designation of "stranger" is fleeting and artificial if you allow it to be. It can be undone by one open heart. Jill and I have been embraced by our *amici Italiano*—despite language differences, they have opened their hearts to us and we have opened ours to them—to the great and lasting enrichment of our lives. I did not know it in those months with Francesco in Seattle, but I was adopting the same approach in welcoming him. We had not met each other, but I would not allow us to remain strangers.

Montefalco

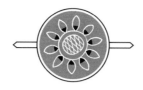

First Days at Cà di Maestro
🌾2004🌾

"Led-d-d-y," I hear from below our steep stairway. The familiar voice of Amedeo. Standing tall on the mosaic stone veranda, he's covered head to toe in moss-green and brown surplus Italian army fatigues. He's on his way to collect mushrooms in the mountains behind our house.

The fit, six foot, fifty-something Cortonese is regarded, without question, as the area expert when it comes to identifying, collecting and even cooking every possible type of local fungi. His schedule as a medical logistics manager for the local hospital district permits him his afternoons searching out the prized porcini. On this sunny April day he's decided I want to accompany him in the woods. What Ame, his common name, forgets is the fungi-fetching stories he's shared with us, several of which included how he creatively used his bamboo stick to keep the viper from biting his well-protected ankles.

"Prossima volta—next time," I say, making a motion to my recovering sinuses.

"Ma stai bene (but you're better now)," he contends.

I sometimes wonder just how much Amedeo's wife, Rosetta, and two daughters Laura and Marianna love seeing the fruits of his passion on the dinner table. Ninety percent of the time Ame exits the woods with at least three dozen mushrooms.

"Next time Ame," and I quickly change the subject to the size and abundance of Cà di Maestro's 60 olive trees.

Living off what nature gives you is how Italians in our little Montanare exist. Sitting on the border of Tuscany and Umbria, this agricultural area yields copious amounts of tomatoes, tobacco, peppers, wheat, sangiovese grapes and, of course, unending olives. Positioned at the end of a three-mile-long valley, the thickly forested hills climb nearly 1500 feet all around us. Like all proud Tuscans, Mr. Mushroom reassures us that everything Tuscan is the best Italy has ever had. He tells us the *lingua pura*, or pure Italian language, is Tuscan. He's just sure Jill and I will speak perfect Italian in no time. We know any improvement above our current set of words will make communication much more efficient. Ame also makes sure we know Tuscan wine, extra virgin olive oil and cured meats from his central Italian region are *migliore*, the best in Italia. His passion for Tuscany's supremacy is evident in the way this middle-aged *simpatico* Ame uses his entire body when making his point. Though having just met us one week earlier, rarely does Ame speak to Jill or me without his right hand firmly planted on our shoulder or forearm. This hands-on approach took a bit of getting used to for us stodgy *americani*. It's one of many contrasts we've learned to love.

Another is living in a house older than our native America.

The life of Cà di Maestro began in 1652 as a single home for fifty people. Its ancient residents must have spent hours gathering wood to keep the stone structure warm.

Upon arrival in Italy in early April, our "must do" list, created by the highly-organized Jill, included "make olive oil". On our first visit to Cà di Maestro we took notice of several dozen trees showing their white spring flowers. *Proprietario* (owner), Piero, was quick to point out that come November we too could be part of the *raccolta* (harvest).

"Vi piace l'orto (you like a garden)?" Piero inquired.

Our minds began to imagine fresh san marzano tomatoes, Italian garlic and basil. "Sì, sì," we said, not stopping to think that we city slickers might lack the necessary green thumbs.

"Vi piace frutta fresca?" He showed us the apple, fig and cherry trees. Having just completed our two week beginning *lingua Italiana* class, we remembered *mela* for apple, *ciliegia* for cherry but *fichi* wasn't one we had covered. We left our pocket-size dictionary in the car so, like with several things in this first month, we did what most people do when they don't get it and said, "Sì, sì."

The presence of the olive trees, the invitation to join the harvest and the oil making, moved the ancient Cà di Maestro up the list as we searched for a permanent home that first spring. But also on our "must do" list was spending a year's worth of days strolling the streets of a medieval village living la dolce vita. Cà di Maestro offered us more than we could have imagined, but we had arrived with a plan and initially we were unwilling to abandon that plan. With rental manifesto and pocket-sized translator in hand, our search for that perfect and quaint village *appartamento* had led us first to the Perugino village of Panicale. Quaint, yes; small, yes. Time needed to walk from one end of the village to the other during the afternoon *passeggiata*: about four minutes including several *buon giornos*.

Fellow American and ex-pat Margaret also sought the refuge of life in a 500-year-old cobblestone street community. In her first year she seemed to have mastered the language, had become a fixture in the village and was aware of every available rental property within 10 miles. Margaret met us for a cappuccino at Bar Centrale. Few things in Italy begin well without espresso. We'd been brought together by online postings of those seeking life at another pace. Our hearts sang as Margaret told us how daily life in Panicale adjusted her way of life to a clip half that of her East-Coast-American pace. We could only hope to experience the same benefit if we could just find the right village dwelling for ourselves.

Margaret took us to see Signora Teresa who, after a brief introduction, jammed a medieval-style key in the weathered steel lock of a thick wooden door like she meant to hurt it. At 6'2", a frame such as mine was not an architectural consideration some five centuries back and I nearly paid for that fact with my head more than once. Climbing the narrow passage up the slightly left-leaning stairs had the feel of entering a tree house. Could we make this listing, bent-over ascent every day for the next year? Using our newly acquired twenty words of Italian, we nervously tried to explain what our body language said so clearly: Panicale would remain a place to visit, not to live.

Just below Panicale is Missiano, home to our next possibility. Alessio, a local architect with a passion for Venetian antiques and a mastery of our native tongue, proudly pointed out the recent improvements to his garden house. As a welcome change he could respond to Jill's carefully written rental inquiries without the normal ambiguity. Everything seemed right about this slice of Tuscan paradise with one exception: Missiano had yet to join the digital revolution. Once Alessio announced his lack of access to the World Wide Web we began a slow shuffle toward the door. We needed to maintain a connection with our families, so this technological limitation was a non-negotiable despite the house's many charms.

As our little Daewoo Matrix rental coasted us off the hill and away from Missiano, I could see my desire to be an Italian farmer at Cà di Maestro might become a reality.

ZONA
TRAFFICO LIMITATO

Cortona

A Little Each Month
🌿2004🌿

Although the late summer sun still kept us plenty warm, by August of our first year the tractors pulling trailers of neatly-stacked wood made us consider what others were obviously planning for—winter. Originally constructed in 1652, Cà di Maestro, the beautiful stone house in which we lived during our first year in Italy, and to which we have returned each year since, once used only wood to keep its 50 residents both warm and fed. Today, after a thorough reconstruction, the four units of Cà di Maestro host pilgrims like us.

Looking back, we laugh when recalling our adventure securing Cà di Maestro as our Italian home. With just two weeks of language class in our brains, leasing a piece of Tuscan paradise from the *proprietario* (owner), Piero, shaded toward becoming a contemporary version of Abbott and Costello's "Who's on First" routine. Jill had done months of research about the kinds of questions we should ask before renting to avoid surprises, misunderstandings and serious pitfalls later on. Among the most important questions requiring answer, Jill learned, was the projected costs of heating whatever home we would be renting. But, if we couldn't get past ciao and *buon giorno*, how in the world

⚜

were we ever going to ask how much we should expect to pay for heat?

Fortunately, our next visit with Piero included friend Francesco who had spent three months learning English in a Seattle college. Our only challenge was that the 25-year-old Cortonese hadn't really spoken our native tongue for about a year. With pocket dictionary in hand, as well as Jill's list of questions, our Vaudeville show continued.

Yes, Piero replied to Francesco, he would order a phone for internet access.

When?

"Mai una linea telefonica in questa casa (this house has never had a telephone line)," he said, almost as if a phone line wasn't really an important part of life.

Jill spun through her trusty dictionary searching for the word for rent. Found it: *affiti*. "Quando si paga l'affito (What day of the month should we pay the rent)?"

"Non ć è un problema. Pagare quando siete comodi (there is no problem, pay when you're comfortable)."

"Quanto costa for heat?"

"Pochi ogni mese (a little each month)."

I love this Italian ambiguity. Jill, on the other hand, needs facts and prefers straight answers. She rarely gives up until she has them. Before leaving, we took one more look, taking note of the exposed beam ceilings, the gigantic matrimonial with four-poster bed, guest room and oversized bathroom. The house was *senza residenti* (without residents) for the previous eight months, so we also noticed the 45-degree temperature. We wondered just how long this really old house with radiator heat would take before we could sit without our GoreTex and fleece. That was a question far outside of our current language skills so we skipped asking.

Cà di Maestro was a clear winner of the handful of places we considered during our one month search. Our original picture of our life in Italy included living as *cittadini*, city people, in a medieval hill town. As we considered life in the country with a garden, a pool, olive trees and plenty of trails in the woods to work off the previous night's pasta, we began to imagine ourselves as *contadini*, country people. But Jill's list of questions was getting longer by the minute. Are we farmers? Do we know how to clean a pool? Who cuts the acre of lawn? Who picks the olives, pears, figs and apples? Will wild animals show up in our yard? Do we need to buy a shotgun? What kind of bugs and snakes live in the country?

With too many questions and no way to ask them or get an answer, we needed to regroup in our tiny bungalow at Parco Fiorito. Our one month there was ending in seven days. The next morning, over a very strong espresso, we shared our twenty question list with Parco Fiorito owner and chef, Roberto Russo. The *Napoli*-born Tuscan convert could see this nice American couple looking for a place to call home for a year could possibly be his worst nightmare if he didn't get us some help soon. He also already had our bungalow rented for the day after we were to leave. On the phone with Piero, Roberto worked through Jill's rental manifesto. The helplessness of not being able to understand the conversation made us uneasy.

Chef Russo hung up the phone, he smiled and said, "tutti bene, everything's alright. You can move in anytime."

I was relieved but, of course, we had one person in need of more information and Chef Russo's answers reflected the same randomness we got 24 hours earlier from Piero. The questions continued.

"Did he say how much the gas and heat would be?"

"Yes, a little each month."

"How much is a little?" Jill insisted, believing there had to be at least a cost range we should expect.

The Chef's answer was classic: "The heat will cost more in the winter."

We returned to our poolside bungalow. It was too early for a glass of wine. I did my best "can't we trust humanity" soliloquy, but Jill wanted answers and time was running short. This was the first real feeling of stress we'd experienced since our arrival three weeks earlier.

Back on the internet, Jill was trying to figure out how much a liter of Italian GPL (natural gas) cost. I went out and talked to Akim, the Parco Fiorito horse.

Cortona

Lavanderia
2004

Italians like things fresh. Laundry is no exception. Open any tourist's photo album and you'll see at least a few snapshots of a cotton rainbow hanging just below shuttered windows. We Americans seem fascinated by this everyday part of Italian fresh living.

This novelty wore quickly at Cà di Maestro. The fact that our next 12 months would be absent a dryer wasn't a surprise. Acquiring a folding clothes line wouldn't be a tough task. In fact, Jill was excited to revisit the way her mother dried clothes when Jill was a child in Michigan. But the bloom came off the country-style laundry rose because of the combined factors of Location and Lack of Knowledge.

The location of the tiny Dyson washer is Jill's least favorite feature of Cà di Maestro. Three hundred steps from our front door, in a wind-worn metal cabana next to the garden, sits our own, personal, rustic laundry shack. Held together by canvas straps, rusty chains and sections of nylon rope, this laundry oasis also requires a long pole wedged in the ground to keep the severely bent door from flapping in the Tuscan wind. Once the hornet nests were cleared, Jill made me promise snakes had taken up residence in other area laundry shacks but not ours.

During one of our many unscheduled linguistic lessons, which just happened to be the day before our planned laundry premiere, Amedeo gave us specific instructions on how to treat a fresh viper bite. Once Jill was completely petrified, he assured us that if one gets to the hospital within 30 minutes, a destiny with death could almost always be avoided. Almost always.

During his weekly adventures in search of porcini, Ame has had plenty of viper encounters. "Yes" was Amedeo's response as to whether the brown, one-foot-long creatures appreciate the environs of Cà di Maestro.

"Certo, ma partiranno quando l'estate arriva (Of course, but they'll leave when summer arrives)."

I smiled. Jill did not.

The little *serpenti* do in fact live in the lowlands until summer arrives. Sometimes I can tell just by looking in Jill's eyes what's coming next. Jill declared her days doing laundry would begin sometime in July, maybe. That plan was confirmed two days later when we almost ran over a slithering viper halfway up Via Vallecchia, our half-mile dirt road.

We would wait until the weather warmed and the snakes moved to the highlands.

When our laundry day did, at last, arrive, we realized we lacked the most basic knowledge: what soap should we use?

Rolling down the laundry aisle of our favorite new grocery store, we once again felt unprepared to complete what just weeks ago we could have done with our eyes shut. Blue soap? Pink soap? White soap? Is it really soap? It smelled like soap. How would we ask? We needed laundry counsel.

Fortunately British ex-pats Bill and Tina, whom we befriended in our basic Italian language class, agreed to make the five-minute commute to The Penny Market. Seeing our confusion, their recommendation was one of each color and a box of small bars to fight off too much iron, magnesium and hydrogen sulfide in the water. Tina carefully explained the amount of each to use, recognizing ours as one of the last nations to master the metric system. With determination and lots of cleaning solutions, we felt equipped for a successful laundry mission.

As we finished and laid the first load of whites in the Tuscan breeze, our sense of accomplishment quickly faded. Four-inch yellow spots covered everything. Without use for several months, the subterranean water line feeding the laundry shack had become full of a thick, yellow, mineral sludge. As I took the first step toward our new neighbors, my brain spun over the question of how I was going to explain our first laundry challenge.

Francesca responded pointing at the hose next to her house and repeating, again and again, "Quel tubo è sporco perché non l'usiamo spesso," telling us that the below-ground hose is dirty because it hasn't been used much.

During our first year, we became quite used to all Italians saying the same word to us at the end of each sentence: "Capito?"

Our rolling eyes and falling shoulders often answered.

Piazzano

The Dirt Road
2004

For the life of me, I couldn't make out what the muffled voice was saying as it came up our half-mile dirt and gravel road. Even as the man's truck-mounted loud speaker got closer to Cà di Maestro, whatever he was offering, I didn't get it.

Via Vallecchia is our Commune-maintained, one-lane, winding road connecting us to the strada. Quick taps on the horn at corners is an unspoken rule we quickly learned coming or going from Cà di Maestro. More often than not, we yield to a troop of chickens roaming from the hen house behind the yellow post office. Halfway up, Giovanni and family raise large white geese. The geese, too, have the right of way on Via Vallecchia. Rarely do they leave the grassy comfort of the sloping vineyards.

It turns out the guy with the microphone in his mouth is selling fruit. In one of our first charades-meets-whodunit sessions with *vicina* (neighbor) Francesca, she explained the man has every fruit and vegetable imaginable. "In supermercato mai," said Francesca, proclaiming she never goes to the supermarket.

We figured as much when she and husband Primo gave us a look around the rustic series of shacks behind their two-story Tuscan-yellow house. Breathing through her mouth to avoid the odor, Jill tried to stay engaged as Francesca took us on our first-ever Italian chicken tour.

"Troppe uova fresche ogni giorno (too many fresh eggs every day)," Francesca said, handing us four each. Warm, large and light brown. I imagined no place could offer me a truer version of fresh.

Around the corner was a caged, lone, white creature with ears the size of my hands and pink eyes. This *coniglio* (rabbit) took first place as the largest I'd ever seen.

"Perché è sola?" I inquired as to why Snow White was alone.

"Questa madre, figli indietro," this was the mother and all the kids were in back. I caught Jill looking at me as she located the 20 or so kids in the back. Her eyes screamed, "I don't eat rabbits!"

"Questo è il padre," Francesca motioned to the jet-black Roger Rabbit, explaining he needed a space far from the rest of the family. "Vi piacciono l conigli?" Francesca asked of our rabbit-eating palate. Having just filled our hands with fresh eggs, I was pretty sure our nice neighbor wasn't going to send us home with a furry little bunny. Although I hadn't actually answered the question Francesca upped the four-legged offer. "Questa domenica, faccio coniglio con potate al rosemarino in forno a legna." The cage before us was to be a bit less crowded after this Sunday. Francesca was cooking in the outdoor wood fired oven and we were invited!

Francesca is always eager to share. Right behind the animal house her beautifully-tilled garden gives about anything one could find in any produce aisle. As the season moves so does the crop of Francesca's *orto*. We often find a large plastic bowl of just-cut lettuce, cucumbers, beans, and carrots resting next to our door. Our first encounter with this bounty-sharing nature was our very first night at Cà di Maestro. Though we hadn't even really met yet, Francesca arrived at our paned wood door with *focaccia rosmarino*, right out of the wood fired oven. Lacking much else, with our green language skills we delivered a dozen *grazies*. With full bellies and warm hearts we knew this special woman would become a most important part of our lives.

Now she had asked us to join her table and I wanted to say yes. But in saying yes, I might force Jill face to face with a plate of *coniglio*. Either I had to lie about an imaginary impending Sunday field trip or use what language I could muster to explain to Francesca and hope she would understand.

"Volentieri, we'd love," I said, accepting the invitation. I felt a familiar foot against my ankle. "Una problema, Francesca," I said, hoping to redeem my outrageous behavior. "Jill mangia solo pollo."

"Non ć è problema." Francesca smiled, motioning to the dozens of fowl jogging the farm.

Firenze

A Car for a Year

☙2004☙

Giuseppe's white VW Golf had been sitting idle next to the barn for at least three years. Chef Roberto's eldest son was much more suited for his Benz upgrade. I imagined Giuseppe's trash becoming my treasure as the one-month term was coming to an end on our Daewoo Matrix roller skate rental car.

Like everything else in our new foreign land, buying a car was going to be an adventure. Between our collective misunderstanding of English/Italian words for different car parts, Roberto and I hatched a plan to get this fine German automobile to Giuliano at the Total Gas station in Montanare, just 2 miles down the road. Jill's vote in favor of this Italian auto deal was all good with just one caveat: She wanted to have an after-market air conditioning system installed. Even the rookie mechanic in me knew this was a tall order.

After Giuliano noted the handful of parts needed to get the car in good working order, I began to explain Jill's desire to explore the Italian road system in climate-controlled comfort. Giuliano's response was purely nonverbal: The motion of rolling down the window was his solution.

"Air Conditioning is a must," was the first thing I heard upon my return. I took to the internet. My inability to differentiate installing *aria condizionata* in a home, factory, or car made my search futile. I took the short jaunt across the beautiful Parco Fiorito courtyard to see Roberto at his 15th-century Venetian desk.

"Disturbo," I said as I entered, trying not to break his rhythm, even though I knew I was.

Roberto is quick to pick up the phone. He called up Total Gas and began a 90-mile-an-hour discussion with Giuliano, the station's resident *officina meccanica.* Between them, they decided our new ride needed to go to the mechanic one hour north in Arezzo, birthplace of Michelangelo.

"Molto caro, Lorenzo," Roberto declared. *It's going to be expensive.*

The mood was tangibly upbeat when I returned to find Jill making dinner. As our family CFO, Jill wanted to know how much. Of course, I hadn't pressed Senore Russo beyond his short remark.

"We'll know a domani," I said, borrowing a useful phrase from nearly every conversation we casually pick up in our daily movements.

Also important to our goal of acquiring this 1.6 liter dream car was liability insurance. Every car, truck, motorcycle, and scooter in Italy must have a valid liability insurance card posted on the windshield. So says one of the few always-enforced Italian Federal Laws. Before that could be achieved, though, we needed one other rather important document known to all as a Code Fiscale. This social security number, of sorts, can be acquired through various means, but is a must for all things financial.

Roberto sensed an afternoon of hand holding was in store. We are reminded of his Italian-Police driving-school-background every time we ride in his leather-upholstered Mercedes Van. This unscheduled trip to the Commune was under his skin and the German six speed transmission was feeling it. The Cypress-lined road between Parco Fiorito and SP 71 is a winding three-quarters of a mile. It was Mr. Russo's opportunity to pilot his Benz like an F1 driver. Jill and I were sure only our Hail Marys could deliver us to our destination in one piece.

Screaming into town, Roberto made a sudden stop in front of the local flower stand. I've learned to never question his intentions. If I stay quiet and watch, I learn something each time about how Italy really works. He reappeared with quite a bouquet and the chances it was for Jill were slim.

Most people enter the Commune office and take a quick inventory of those waiting. With two benevolent *americani* in tow, our Neapolitan guide edged his way to the side and extended his hand to the woman across the counter with the flowers still behind him. When their hands touched, the flowers appeared and Roberto's lips met her hand. The scene was appreciated by all but loved by few as we had just hijacked the 20 people waiting.

Covered in a navy blue Fendi dress with equally stylish tan Prada pumps, Monica, the object of Roberto's wooing, had the proper documents in order within five minutes and reveled in the floral arrangement. As the Silver van left the unpaid parking stall, Vivaldi's *Primavera* poured from the speakers. I learned later, that is Mr. Russo's victory song.

Next, we entered the office of Vittorio Accioli, Roberto's business partner in more than one endeavor, as well as the father of Francesco and the elder Alessandro. He happens to also be the agent for Lloyd Adriatico, our soon-to-be liability insurance carrier. With less of a grand entrance we met Rosetta, another Italian gal with good taste in high fashion labels. With her skinny, white cigarette burning in the ashtray, she began asking questions, none that we could decipher though. Once the formalities were covered, using Roberto as a translator, she inquired of our desires to be in Italy for one year. Every answer seemed to lead to a greater sense of curiosity. I began to understand where these inquiries were coming from. Rosy is much more than the office manager here. She is the keeper of all family matters as well. Her three decades minding the store helped hold a family together through it all, including an Italian marital separation, as divorce was not a legal possibility. Information is her equity and Rosy keeps it close to the vest.

Rosy, wearing Ferrari-red lipstick, placed before me a scrap of paper with a number while she enjoyed a last drag of a butt. Italian insurers expect full payment before issuing coverage. My stack of Euros left Rosy a bit extra. After all, she wasn't running a change operation. My nonverbal was all she needed to acknowledge the remaining was hers. The dot matrix printer spit out a three-part document. Rosy tried to be professional and read aloud the details but noticed the glaze covering my chestnut eyes. "Andiamo," Roberto declared and off we went with insurance in hand.

The suggested *limita veloce* on Via Piele back to Parco Fiorito is 50 km per hour. I've learned Roberto's goal is always double. Vivaldi's *Primavera* blaring on the CD player provided divine protection on Chef Russo's public racetrack back to Piazzano. Our morning walks include this same pavement. With enhanced vigilance, I often take notice if the Grey Speed Wagon is in its parking space before seeking a bit of exercise.

Now, with our paperwork in order, I set out in the Golf. Not a fan of Italian roads or the natives that occupy them, Jill trails me in the Daewoo to a destination we have never been. Arezzo feels like a college town. If you aspire to be an architect of restored structures dating back several centuries, you will have spent some time learning that craft in Arezzo. Giorgio Vasari, the accomplished mentor of Michelangelo, is honored well on many inscriptions including Piazza Grande, the most important *città centro*.

Should you have challenges with traffic circles, you best avoid this provincial capital of Tuscany. They were not designed for the person following you, no matter your comfort level. I decide to go around again, trusting the little Daewoo would follow. Italians are not afraid to use the middle of the steering wheel to sound their disgust with another visitor. We round the circle, then off down the street to the mechanic.

As at other service businesses we've had the pleasure of visiting, we are at a loss to find anyone working. A stout and crazy-curled white-haired man is leaning on the building enjoying a Marlboro forty feet from the door I just walked through. He knows I'm here but his pleasure is not to be disturbed just yet. He drags a few more times on the cigarette and then approaches.

"Sono Lorenzo, amico di Giuliano," I declare, as if we've been pals forever.

"Sì," as he points at our German super car. "Sicuro?" He shoots back asking if we're sure we want to add a feature to this car that will cost more than the car is worth.

There's an international nonverbal sign among men when something defies logic but must be done: Lowering my head with a slight angle at Jill, out of the corner of my mouth comes, "Sicuro."

"Venerdì (Friday)." He tosses my keys to the desk.

Siena

Soccer, Taxes, and Fiorentina vs. Inter Milano
❦2004❦

Although Tuscans are surrounded by culture on four sides, only sports and politics rule the exchanges of senior men who gather outside Italian coffee bars. Using our four ears, Jill and I have done enough "exit polling" to verify this national reality.

Throughout Italy, the most widely circulated daily paper is the 50-page pink Gazzetta dello Sport. Perhaps it's no mistake this daily publication's line between sports and politics is nonexistent. The normally well-dressed seniors simultaneously debate how Silvio Berlusconi's plan to extend the retirement age for benefits will affect the outcome of next week's match between Fiorentina and Torino-based arch rival Juventus. Although strange to us Nikon-toting Americans, sports and specifically soccer, appears to unite the most opposite political foes. In a country with eight major political parties, sports create a needed link between neighbors. Our Italian wish list included seeing and feeling this passion for ourselves.

Amedeo mentioned "his" *squadra cuore* was playing a home game against Inter Milano. Even I, the most passive soccer fan, knew this was to be a *grande partita*, a big game. Italian men each support their own team. Each chooses his team at an early age and

❧

it's well understood he will stand behind his team regardless of its place in the current standings. During one of many unforgettable outdoor Sunday feasts, our visiting Roman friend Alessandro, put it in words we could understand: "You can change your job, your girlfriend, your house and even your Vespa, but you never, ever, change your soccer team." His short dissertation explains why Amedeo has Fiorentina soccer blood pumping from his *cuore*.

The wind was howling from the north when we arrived at Fiorentina's home stadium. Our first charge was finding tickets. Those available to the public went quickly. Because scalping carries a stiff penalty, the only way to identify those hawking tickets is by looking for men holding wads of cash. Ame disappeared around the corner. It felt like a high school pot buy. A short time later, Ame returned with prize in hand. For about $50 each, two times the face value, we were the proud owners of three seats in the section known as Curva Fiorentina.

Like most things relating to organization, Italians don't see the need to occupy the seats that correspond with the numbers on the tickets. Although I'm more than OK with this method, my well-organized Capricorn Jill felt we would soon be asked to leave. Still we proceeded hoping for the best.

Prompted by the roar of fans still outside the D-shaped stadium, we turned around and witnessed the first of many highly unusual sights involving several dozen riot police. The only way to keep the Fiorentina *tifosi* (fans) from starting a street war with visiting fans from Milan is by providing the milanesi a police escort to the *contro*—away— team section. Once the noisy milanesi cleared the pat-down and bag-search area, they were slowly escorted to a special section surrounded by a twenty-five-foot security fence. If that wasn't enough, a member of the riot squad was placed every three feet to prevent opposing fans from taunting each other through the three-story fence. Pointing at the front mounted camera, Ame nonchalantly explained the blue Police Helicopter now circling the *stadio* just 500 feet above was photographing the entire audience should a major riot break out.

"Do you think we're safe here?" Jill whispered, a rather worried look suffusing her freezing red face. I couldn't respond with a confident "yes". I looked around and pointed out the nearest exit should a quick getaway be necessary.

After a pre-game children's match, all 50,000 Fiorentini stood and shouted anthems meant to rile the opposing fans. With the air full of pre-game angst, the caged Inter-Milano fans began unrolling large paper banners describing the sexual preferences of the Fiorentina coach's wife. Mayhem broke out with Fiorentina's first goal. The well-armed polizia did everything to keep the home fans from scaling the fence. Minutes later, Inter returned the scoring favor. Once again, the crazed behavior but this time coming from inside the cage. Even after a pat down, metal detector, and bag search, a dozen crazed fans had been able to enter with road flares. One blazed to life now. As the burning red rocket flew from the only open part of the cage I could see, its trajectory was on course for the seats 20 rows below us. Seconds later and to the dismay of police just 30 feet away, the glowing flame was returned to its original launch pad. Short of some slightly burned clothing, everyone survived the moment.

Amedeo was disappointed with the 1-1 result. It wouldn't move Fiorentina ahead in the *Classifica Italia*, the barometer of all Italian soccer pride. The match concluded, Ame guided us back to calmer waters, Jill and I feeling as if we'd just survived a bloody drive-by shooting.

European soccer has serious political facets too.

For tonight's match, we gather outside Ame and Rosy's 4th floor Mansardo residence aside a long set of green outdoor tables with a 50-inch Sony blaring the lineup of Italy vs. Germany. The winner must face Spain in the final on Sunday night. Most realistic soccer fans would agree Spain is the world's best. The two UEFA Cups in the past three seasons say so.

The gigantic terra cotta *terrazza* faces south with an incredible vista to the end of the Val di Chiana. A breezy 85-degree June evening, the full moon ascends behind the church, Chiesa di Sepoltaglia, as if part of a Broadway set. Situated atop the highest hill next to Lake Trasimeno, this was the strategic gathering spot for Hannibal's decimation of 15,000 Roman troops in 217 B.C. He let his enemy gather adjacent the shore and within four hours the victory was clinched. Jill and I once hiked the rugged three mile trail from Piazzano. It's obvious why this would be a superior place to note every movement of an incoming force.

Our focus is called to the teams about to take the field. Ame looks my way, "Speriamo," he says looking over his rimless glasses with his hands in a prayerful position. In an effort to bridge both generations, each player steps afield holding hands with a uniformed child. UEFA, the sport's governing body, has taken complex measures to increase the respect among team players. Via the stadium's public address system, each team captain recites his side's commitment to respect. Even the player's left arm sleeve hosts a RESPECT patch.

Tonight's match in Kiev represents much more than soccer. These are trying times in Europe's financial experiment, the European Union. It all seemed like such a good idea: Let each member continue to drive its own economy, preserve its culture, enjoy an open set of borders, all the while using a common currency issued by a central bank. Like with many other big ideas, however, someone is bound to end up in the ditch. With minimal changes to the litany of massive legacy costs and little GDP growth, several Euro Zone nations are hamstrung in the economic competition—they are squads playing with multiple yellow cards. Although Rome's political machine would like the world to think otherwise, Milan, home to the Borsa Italiana trading markets, has seen the light; its economic forecast appears stormy at best. Like the states, Italy has a revenue challenge. Those sporting Ferraris, Lamborghinis, Mercedes, and *alta moda* clothing, contribute little to the common cause.

For Ame and most of his legit-income-generating friends, la dolce vita has a negative trickle-down effect. Once, sitting outside the busy Camucia Gelateria, enjoying a mid-day escape from the 90-degree sunshine, Ame explained the economics. It sounded identical to our front-page news, but actually with less hope. Ame hung his head and laid down some facts: Both his and Rosy's income is public record. There's no wiggle room when paying taxes. Motioning to a passing shiny new green Jag, Ame declares of the comfortable driver, "Lui non paga le tasse (he pays no taxes)." Even though La Guardia Finanza has an entire army of inspectors in charge of money flow, Ame and Rosy must pay 65 cents of every euro they earn to cover those flying below the tax man's radar. In light of Italy's place in the EU doghouse, the forecast for Ame isn't bright. Rome has proposed new measures pushing his obligation north of 70 cents.

Although benefits include lifetime healthcare and a nominal retirement pension, it's what remains that keeps a smile on Ame's youthful 60-year-old face. He knows his generation must shoulder the pain. For daughters Marianna and Laura, father hopes for better Euro weather. They too have chosen work that dictates a serious subtraction of taxes. Marianna, a mid-thirties former model, her husband Luca and her sister Laura each spend their work days in support of U.S. companies including Guess, Nike, and Calvin Klein.

Nearly 10 years ago, a half dozen U.S.-style outlet malls sprang up, with tenants sporting mostly New York brands. It's no coincidence the majority of shoppers are hardly Italiano. Of equal beauty as her sister, Marianna, and eight years younger, Laura tells me about busloads of eager buyers from Asia, America, and Russia, each in love with American brands. From my observation, they appreciate Rome and Paris fashion houses too. For those with a wallet full of discretionary Euros, it's the perfect shopping storm. Laura has dreams beyond the EU and her jeans showroom. Her California visit a year ago put her ethos wheels in motion. For husband want-to-be, long-term boyfriend, Stefano, whose well-known Tuscan wine producer Antinori scheduled the Golden State visit, Laura's new-found love of all things American could be his worst nightmare.

Minutes prior to kick off now Rosy decides I need another helping of Ame's *bucatini all'amatriciana*. The pasta recipe from the hills just north of Rome has enough Calabrese peperoncino to make a man sweat, even without the summer temperature. Italy's national anthem stirs those around me into a frenzy. My appreciation for this important set of notes grew out of watching many late-night podium presentations as Michael Schumacher accepted awards during his seven world-champion seasons at Ferrari. Red wine tops the glasses. The match, Italy's great chance to knock off the EU watchdog, begins. From Ame's giant veranda, in every direction, the sound of an excited nation is palpable. The anticipation is more of a collective opportunity to vindicate a people being trashed in the international media.

It takes only five minutes for Mario Balotelli to perfectly time his header past Germany's expert goalie. Cheering, yelling, crying. I'm reminded how little personal space exists. Balotelli peels his shirt and stands in a stoic pose at mid field. A new look is defined for sports media marketers. Chilled prosecco fills plastic cups. Although another 85 minutes remains, a victory celebration is underway.

Try as they might, with plenty of first-half well-played chances, Germany cannot get one past Italy's super goalie, Buffon. Germany leaves the field at half time with heads hanging and the camera stays with Germany's coach demonstrating his disappointment as his star player avoids eye contact. Rosy takes this pause to deliver a table full of chicken *saltimbocca marsala* and *vedure ripiene*. Her passion is more culinary than sport. She's in favor of Ame's spiritual connection to soccer but sees it more as a time for him to be with the guys.

Folding two sage leaves and a healthy slice of speck inside an oval piece of flat chicken, Rosy uses a healthy dose of marsala wine during the final minute of perfection. Her stuffed peppers and zucchini are an incredible compliment. We've been the beneficiary of Rosy's and Ame's *cucina Italiana* on many occasions. It's a miracle I can fit into an economy class airplane seat after weeks of Rosy's mastery. She greets the table with a tray offering more. I rarely pass.

Luca and Marianna arrive as foot meets ball for the second half. Germany wants blood. Apparently the animated pep talk that began at the end of the first half has the German side believing their entire country thinks they can make it happen tonight. *Gli Azzurri* pick up on this new enthusiasm and bring their best in response. Each skilled pass is matched with an equal hustle to steal the specially designed UEFA Cup black-and-white ball. All are now standing. This game is too intense for a casual stance. Ame, Luca, and I, among others, offer high-volume advice to the Sony wide screen.

I hear the same raucous counsel coming from verandas all around us.

A long pass giving Germany its best look is ruled offside. It's pandemonium in Ukraine and all over Italy. More prosecco is passed and no one cares about its room temperature except caring host Rosy. Another arrives cold. Foil is gone in seconds and the cork jets 20 feet to the stars. A long cross-field pass leaves Italy plenty of ball and field to set up a center pass. Two charging Germans cannot match the Italian ball-handler's pace. Germany's goalie anticipates his isolation but is left with only one option. The Italian closes. From 20 feet, he launches a rocket. All of Italy erupts seeing the ball fill the back of the net. A mid-field celebration commences once the Italian hero finishes a sprint parade to each corner of the field. Our dozen are mostly in tears. Italy is 10 minutes away from playing Spain for the most important trophy in European Soccer. Beyond the World Cup, not much else defines soccer success like the UEFA Cup.

Rosy seizes this celebratory moment to deliver this special-event dolce. Chilled sliced peaches, with a hint of sugar, soaked in red wine for two days is a terrific last course. A clear, slender glass bottle of Rosy's house-made limoncello hits the table. Never needing to be told again, my eye knows the perfect spot on the plastic cup to say when. One overdose of limoncello per lifetime is all I can handle.

Germany once again presses to no avail. It is as if we needed a purpose to down our *digestivi*. Italy responds with another long pass but slows to let the play develop. Moving the ball in a triangle, Italy patiently awaits a hole in the defense, a major strong suit for Germany. A long angle kick from nearly the corner.

A German head intercepts but doesn't clear. A swinging left foot takes advantage. The ball spins into the German net and the screams continue.

Having never consumed prosecco at the end of a meal, I'm still not in favor of such a move but couldn't help myself under the festive circumstances. Even as the referee adds four minutes of extra time, the deal is done. Italy has overcome more than a well-prepared foe. This is a feel-good evening for a country tried in the media as a place unable to compete and win. Few will argue its failing economic model, but on this night Italy has taken on Big Brother and come out on top.

Le Celle

Vaticano Natale
🌾2004🌾

*A*uguri is the salutation Italians use to wish each other well during celebrations and holidays. Merchants throughout towns big and small hang neon Auguris in their store-fronts during the Christmas season. Even Vera at our little coffee shop began adding "Auguri" to the familiar "Ciao".

The Christmas lights strung through Castiglion Fiorentino made an already quaint medieval hill town even more festive. The birthplace of actor Roberto Benigni, the family of Dean Martin, and our good friend Amedeo, Castiglion also makes claim to Castello di Montecchio. The perfectly restored 14th-century castle sports a 250 foot *albero di Natale* (Christmas tree). With its point at the castle, the lit tree outline follows the gentle hill to its base.

"Questo, il più grande albero di Natale in Toscana," Amedeo said, proudly telling us this is the biggest Christmas tree in Tuscany. He, wife Rosy and daughter Laura could see the wonder in our eyes as we stood in the freezing Tuscan night. In America, we're used to lit TV towers and illuminated trees in shopping centers, but a 600-year-old magnificent hilltop Christmas castle reminded us this was to be a season to remember.

Posters outside local businesses promoted community *presepi* (nativity scenes), masses, and concerts. Neighboring Pietria hosts a *Presepio Vivo*, a live nativity. The familiar commercialism and anxiety accompanying Christmas in America is absent. Instead, there exist feelings of calm and collective thanks.

"Che cosa fai per Natale?" Francesco inquired wanting to know our plans for Christmas Day. We had a good idea this invitation for a 2 PM post-Christmas lunch with his mother Fiorella, 84-year-old nonna (grandmother) Anita and brother Alesandro would be memorable.

"Nonna is making her annual hand-rolled tortellini."

"Volentieri—we'd love to," Jill accepted.

Before Jill, Christmas at home in America had fallen into a routine for me. For the past several years the Christmas Eve ritual had been: shop till they kick me out of the store, wrap the presents with my mom while listening to the soundtrack to *A Charlie Brown Christmas*, try to go to mass (time permitting), but always end up watching the tape-delay of midnight mass from Vatican City. It was my Christmas wish every year to one day stand in Saint Peter's Square to hear Pope John Paul II say that midnight mass of Christmas.

I, therefore, had great anticipation about *vigilia di Natale*, this Christmas Eve, in Italy. This year my Christmas vision was coming true.

Jill and I boarded a noon intercity train for Rome on December 24th to realize this dream of a lifetime. Excitement and joy filled my soul as we rumbled south towards the eternal city. Having made this trip many times, this was the first time we'd have to stand the entire trip. This train's final destination was Napoli. Every student, son, daughter, aunt and uncle was headed home for the holidays.

Mother Nature welcomed us to Roma with a compliment of driving rain and enough wind to make umbrellas dangerous. Our accommodation for the night was filled with other westerners in search of a spiritual holiday experience. Despite the challenging weather, Piazza Navona was full of finely-dressed Romans patronizing dozens of Christmas market stalls. This busy Piazza, once host to chariot races some 1700 years ago, is now the place patrons come to buy *La Strega di Befana*: The Witch of the January 6th Epiphany is the character in Italian folklore that decides who's been naughty or nice. Having one or two hanging around your house is apparently a good way to keep order.

White lights from Hotel Pantheon added an illumination to the oldest dome in the world. Even at 8 PM on Christmas Eve, flocks filled the resting place of Victor Emmanuelle II and Raphael. Bar Michillania is an obligatory stop for us when in Rome. For 25 years, Miki has welcomed *i stranieri* from literally all over the world, as evidenced by the college banners from Brisbane to UCLA. Miki was standing out front when we arrived. He invited us to come back in an hour for a special meal with his friends. As each of the five courses arrived and another glass of wine poured, our table of twenty-five said another *salute*. Ahmed, a dinner guest from Egypt, explained Miki does this dinner each year for those who haven't another place to celebrate.

Keeping an eye on the time, we bid everyone, including Roman, Miki's adopted Romanian son, a final *Buon Natale* and began our pilgrimage across Rome. Crossing the Tiber at Ponte San Angelo, I began experiencing feelings of deep gratitude and peace. I took Jill's hand just as she began to explain a tangible spirit in the air. As we rounded the back of the fortified castle named for an angel, the quarter mile Via della Conciliazione filled our eyes. There, bathed in lights, the Basilica San Pietro.

Even after visiting Città del Vaticano a dozen times, I continue to experience that profound emotion which only deep respect and faith can bring. Standing there, my feet are rooted on the very ground that my faith is based upon. I give much of the credit for my good fortune in life to my faith. Returning to its source is a renewal each time.

As our feet set on Piazza San Pietro, my dream of hearing Pope John Paul II say Christmas Mass was about to actualize. Sharing this momentous and soulful night with Jill only added to the texture of my feelings. In the center of Saint Peter's Square stood a gigantic presepio and a fifty-foot fir, lit from top to bottom. With several thousand worshipers braving the elements, we carefully listened to each word the Pope said, hoping to at least understand the subject matter. Everything about this mass was beautiful and nearly surreal. Voices from the Vatican choir and the ringing of the bells filled Saint Peter's Square. Behind Pope John Paul II, in familiar purple, assembled the Council of Cardinals. Between biblical readings, international children dressed in native costume presented gifts to the 84-year-old ailing pontiff. Even though Parkinson's has limited his ability to express himself, John Paul's eyes glistened receiving them all.

Back home in Seattle I would be glued to my screen, the warm but quiet air of my home surrounding me and accentuating my distance from this scene I now found myself a part of. I would strive for connection with the Pontiff, with his words, with the spirit of the night. It would be a struggle in the midst of so much other pressing responsibility. But this night, here I was, finally. The cold night air of Rome, the warmth and comfort of Jill beside me sharing this moment, the collective reverence of the thousands of faithful gathered with us, and the prospect of Christmas Day with new friends who had opened their hearts to us in this land that was opening our own hearts filled me with joy.

Buon Natale, indeed. Buon Natale.

Venezia

Coffee Here, Coffee There

Jim and I chat Hockey, a childhood sport I still relish but, as a grownup, only observe to avoid spending time rehabbing my aging joints. Our 7 AM banter is brief, as a line forms six sleepy bodies deep. Meg wants to share a feature from her weekend as I steam nonfat for her decaf beverage of choice. Commercial Real Estate magnate Chris expresses his gratitude for connecting him with a private banker friend that can offer special assistance to his youngest son. Our fearless leader, Heather, reminds me to work and entertain in unison as the line is now well into double digits.

Coffee Shop America has been part of my early mornings since I joined Starbucks in 2005. Howard Schultz's wild dream is another significant coincidence in my soul's glue to Italia. On my first non-academic trip to Italy, while perusing Chef Russo's 16th-century stone bookshelf, which I'm sure once held holy relics, I leafed through the first writings of Starbucks' lead evangelist, *Pour Your Heart into It: How Starbucks Built a Company One Cup at a Time*. Within two days, I had consumed every word. Though I had never met the man, I quickly realized we were brothers in coffee and la dolce vita.

My debt to Howard Schultz is enormous. His childhood experiences without quality health care coverage helped define the core values of today's hugely admired global coffee endeavor. Following our year together in Italy, when it became clear that Jill and I had been delivered a miracle and would change our titles from co-entrepreneurs to mom and dad, I sought to enhance our benefits package, which was weak at best. The discarded vacation book I had raced through would become a roadmap to my insurance goal. As a business owner, I found it nearly impossible to believe a major corporation could offer a 20-hour-a-week employee the same peace-of-mind health care package as one that sweats it out full time. A decade of early mornings later, my gratitude continues and my cappuccino skill set has matured.

A decade's worth of journeys to Italy has blessed me, too, with a better understanding of the cultural origins of my craft.

In Camucia, a Tuscan village on the busy SP 71 between Lake Trasimeno and Arezzo, that original craft is on dazzling display. Master barista Fabrizio works the counter at Bar Snoopy in Camucia. His benefits package looks nothing like the benefits I so gratefully receive from Starbucks. His days are double my clock hours, and at just 28 years old, he's the captain of this hugely popular bar situated amongst 500 apartments. Be it 7 AM or 7 PM, his bar is jammed with the young and not-so-young. His five parking spots somehow host 20 Fiats, Ducatis, Vespas and Apes. The spotless white Carrara marble countertop hosts two stainless steel La Marzocco manual espresso machines that always seem to have a cappuccino or doppio order underway. Fabrizio's three 20-something, tan and well-socialized Italian beauties keep the clientele from having to wait. Our friendship over cappuccinos coincides with my decade-long love affair with Montanare. Young Fabrizio worked the counter at Piero and Luisa's always-busy Bar Girasole Gelateria, next to the Co-Op grocery store, a short hop from his current post. Jill and I were beneficiaries of Piero's frozen treats delivered to Cà di Maestro in a white Styrofoam container every other evening—a fact my waist began to reveal soon enough. *Stracciatella*, *fragole*, *limone*, and *cocoa*, all became unintended obsessions. After 30 days of growth, I was finally able to demonstrate my need to quit and Piero began offering extras from the garden instead.

It's not a wonder Mr. Schultz fell for the aura of an Italian coffee bar and hoped to export this way of business to the New World. Locals and family clans visit their favorite spots up to five times a day. Cappuccinos in the morning, doppios in the afternoon, a quick bite of lunch and *aperitivos* after work. If one was to measure and bottle the human energy in Bar Snoopy, and the thousands of other gathering spots like it, most Italians would have no power bill. The common threads include conversations about soccer scores, political scandals, family events, and how the economics of the EU are being handled by the "Wizard of Oz in Germany".

Fabrizio's patrons, like most Italians, are informed. They scan regional and national newspapers strewn about the coffee bar and the comments fly. Unabashedly leaning one way or the other, each paper has its most ardent readers. Italy's most admired daily is the pink Gazzetta dello Sport, a fifty page nirvana for those in every demographic. Although I comprehend little of the editorial writing, this is the publication I seek. For my passion and interest in Formula One is always featured on the final few pages, and I can be one of the Italian crowd reading and watching as Piero, Luisa, daughter Sara, and employee Fabrizio each give the crowd what they need. At this mid-morning hour, Jill is shopping next door and the bar is loaded with late-30's moms and a set of men whose birthdates must have been prior to the First World War. Luisa is keeping pace with the gals as she simultaneously crafts four cappuccinos. Apparently, one of the husbands stayed out a bit late and Luisa isn't shy about sharing her feelings of disapproval. Piero is offering endorsement of a farm-related subject that gets lost in my mental translation.

Much of Starbucks' stateside re-creation of Coffee Shop Italia adds to my gratitude for the old country. Howard's desire to construct a place not of home or office has come true. I'm intrigued and enthused when I see a local business man hosting a two-hour gathering at the long wood trestle table surrounded with old-world bent-wood chairs. Of equal satisfaction, I'm overjoyed when an absent regular reappears with cell phone photos of her new baby. Days spent in Coffee Shop America are some of my best days because I stand with one foot in each world, the old and the new. Howard and I both know the coffee shop is much more than a place just to get caffeinated.

Cortona

Culture Crossroad

2004

Our small five-student language class was held on the fourth floor of an 800-year-old building without built-in heat above Piazza della Repubblica, Cortona's center square. Jill and I came to realize our brains function well even when our toes are turning blue. In the adjacent room sat another five students taking in the advanced version of Italiano. What we would give to possess those skills, we thought. With a total enrollment of two Germans (regarded as *tedesci* by Italians), three Brits, three americani, an Aussie and a Maltese, our school looked like last November's issue of National Geographic.

"Would you two like to stop by our house for a cupper?" advanced student Tina asked with her thick Manchester accent.

For me a cupper was an important piece of protection gear from my days as a hockey player. Fortunately, Jill understood this to be a British request to join them for a cup of afternoon tea at Villa Donato, Bill and Tina's lovely Tuscan hillside home in nearby Ossaia.

"Volentieri (we'd love to)," Jill agreed, using a word acquired in class just ten minutes earlier.

"What can we bring?" I asked trying to be a courteous future guest.

Once the question left my lips I realized that afternoon tea doesn't really require the guest bring anything. Thank God the British don't subscribe to the idea that a stupid question deserves a stupid answer.

With another school day past and our minds swimming in gray matter sludge, we shot down the hill from Cortona to Parco Fiorito, the charming holiday farm we called home for our first 30 days in Tuscany. "Buon giorno, Signor Russo," I tried to the farm's flamboyant owner.

"Perfetto—ora parli italiano (perfect, now you're speaking Italian)!" This is where learning a new tongue can be the most challenging. Our brains want so badly to remember what we've just learned 20 minutes ago. "Piano, Piano (take it slow)," the fifty-something Napolitano suggested.

Navigating the thin road between Piazzano and Ossaia, our 93 VW Golf made the slow uphill climb past the cemetery. I relished the opportunity to pilot the machine anytime Jill says let's go. Jill was still getting used to my philosophy that driving in Italy is based on momentum. No other reasoning could be used to explain the total disregard for posted speed limits, traffic lights and most of all, those waiting for crosswalks. I followed suit— when in Rome, after all (or, in this case, Tuscany).

"How much milk do you take in your tea Larry?" Bill asked.

Milk in tea? "Just a touch, please," I said, wondering if milk was the proper British substitute for the American idea of adding sugar.

Tuscany hosts a large ex-pat community of Brits, Scandinavians, Dutch, Germans and Americans, each adding their unique customs to daily life. Most use Tuscany as a second home escape from what we believe to be a frenetic lifestyle similar to that of our homeland. On any given day we see European

Union license plates from as many as half a dozen different countries. For most western Europeans, including several new friends from Rotterdam and Munich, Tuscany is just 12 hours by car. Some jump in their Audis to ski in the Dolomites Monday, and drink brunello in Montalcino on Tuesday.

"Do you have plans on November 10th?" Tina asked. "If the weather cooperates this is the day we plan la raccolta."

Oh no, I thought quietly, another local word we haven't learned yet. Perhaps the blank canvas of my face was a dead giveaway. Fortunately Bill said, "The picking of the olives."

"Of course we'll help! Volentieri!" I smiled at Jill as I imagined checking off another line on our Must-Do-While-in-Italy list.

Once we made our move to Montanare, I began studying the 60 olive trees in the one acre of park at Cà di Maestro. I also took notice of olive trees everywhere else on our daily trek to and from Cortona. No two are even close to the same. Many stand just tall enough it would seem that a ladder would be in order. But there are no ladders in sight anywhere.

"Sopra, Sopra," Piero answered pointing up at a set of trees next to the pool.

"Senza scala?" I inquired about reaching the tops of those trees without a ladder.

"Certo (sure)."

"Comé prendili (how do you pick them)?" I shot back. After the third round of explaining, I understood him to say one of us would climb the center trunk and straddle the two main branches while another shook the tree. The international sign for shaking something is unmistakable. My imagination started painting a picture of me with a neck brace, crutches, and a cast on my arm. Reentering our two-room slice of Tuscan heaven,

I didn't have the heart to tell Jill that her 5'3" stature made for the perfect tree-hanging olive picker.

I became even more enthralled with how someone was going to get olives off the trees on the 25-degree slopes next to the switch backs going up to Cortona. The climb from the bottom of the Val di Chiana to Cortona is another chance for me to enhance my Formula One driving skills. I find I'm hardly the only one, including the Ducatis that pass with the slightest room for error. God must lay a large and caring hand on Italian drivers. Large doses of divinity are the only hope they have, based on what I witness every time I'm behind the wheel of our speedy VW Golf.

Similar to other 1500-year-old Tuscan villages, Cortona created a good-sized parking lot just below the wall and installed *scala mobile*, today's version of an escalator. The contrast of a sleek steel-and-chrome moving sidewalk while entering a village that dates back to the age of Troy is quite amusing. I never tire of strolling Via Nazionale, Cortona's main commercial walkway. Daniela has lots friends on this street, many who remember watching her bounce around in a stroller as I navigated the thick cobblestones. We would never pass by Lena's shop, which was Cortona's first internet café, where Jill spent hours in recent years seeking a secure and acceptable pace to the World Wide Web. It's a rare occasion that Daniela leaves her gift section without something Lena wants Daniela to have, gratis.

Making our way into Piazza Reppublica, Cortona's main square, another stop and special friend is Ivan Botanci at Galleria il Pozzo. Few people we've met in Italy are more invested in their community than Ivan. His nearly perfect English is another reason we gravitate his way. Daniela freely walks throughout his two-level gallery in search of the six-foot, slender, middle-aged Tuscan.

Only on rare occasions does he turn down her request to feed the gold fish in his glass enclosed 12th-century well.

Ivan too, has an olive grove. He became my next source of olive knowledge and could feel my enthusiasm for accepting the invitation I'd received to gather the olives come fall. Ivan described the attributes of the lucky picker that gets to shimmy the trees on the steep slopes. I realized Jill fit the bill again.

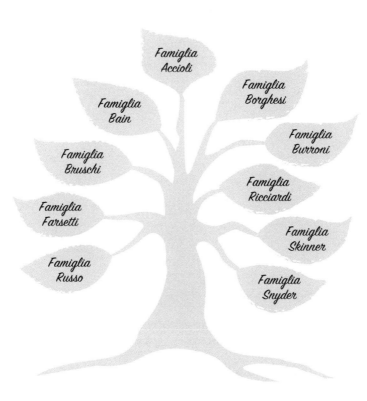

Family Tree of Friendship ~ Ten Years, Ten Families
(There are no biological family relation.)

Ossaia

Extra Virgin Olive Pickers
2004

Piero tells me some of the five dozen Olive trees around Cà di Maestro have been there for 200 years. With split trunks and branches living what appears to be a life of their own, the flat, silvery small leaves glisten even under the hottest Tuscan sun.

Although the making of olive oil was on the Must-Do-While-in-Italy list, Jill and I never actually contemplated how these little nuggets would become that golden treasure we generously spread on freshly-toasted rosemary bread.

"Quando si raccolgono le olive per produrre l'olio (when do the olives become oil)?" I inquired during Piero's ritual morning watering of the roses just outside our front door.

Pointing the flowing hose at the largest tree in sight, "Prima novembre per mangiare." I got everything, but needed some clarity around the eating part. The two largest trees, one under which I've spent countless days escaping the heat, produce the olives we eat. Dropping the running hose, Piero uses his well-worn hands to explain how the olives are placed in an air tight glass cylinder with water and baking soda until they become a condiment on the Christmas table.

As he hydrated the purple irises next to the six-foot stone wall, the question I'd hoped for came my way. "A prima dicembre noi raccogliamo le olive per olio. Anche voi?" Knowing this was near the top of our Bucket List Italiano, I sauntered back inside and shared this olive-oil-making opportunity with Jill. I'm not much of a "how" man, so many of her questions go unanswered, especially the ones that involve a foreign language.

In just two days, we now have two invitations to help produce the world's finest olive oil, even though we have no real idea just how this would go down. Yields year-to-year fluctuate wildly depending on rain fall, infestation, and, in Piero's words, *fortuna grande*. I'm grateful he sees luck as part of his life's work as well.

I began seeking the answers to all Jill's pending questions. It turns out everyone in Tuscany and Umbria is involved in peddling oil in one way or another. It takes nearly every able-bodied man and woman available to get the olives from the tree to the olive press within 24 hours of being picked.

As the season moved on, I had a renewed interest in the tree that kept me cool. Table olives are three times the size of those which become oil. They also keep a lime green color, whereas those that become liquid show a shade resembling army fatigues. Sitting beneath the shady pergola at Villa Donato, Bill filled in the rest of my inquiries. Those off-white nets hanging among the spider webs in Piero's beat up metal cabana had an important purpose come late fall. Putting down his cup of tea, our favorite Brit explained just how we'd get each olive from the branch to the waiting net spread beneath each of five dozen trees. Grateful to have these details covered in our native tongue, my questions continued. Bill assured us there would be plenty of on-the-job training.

The *raccolta* (gathering of olives) at Villa Donato is also a family get-together. Bill and Tina's blended family travel from

Great Britain and Denmark to be part of the annual production of this Tuscan gold in a bottle.

As the leaves turned and fell I started noticing stacks of plastic bins around the olive groves, including the 15 acres next to Francesca's giant yellow house. Mowers were busy cutting the grass beneath each tree to give the nets an even surface. Brisk mornings gave way to sunny afternoons and Mother Nature was suggesting our time was near.

Following double cappuccinos at Vera's miniature coffee shop in Montanare, our mighty white VW Golf climbed the steep one lane of pavement past the Ossaia Cemetery and Campo Sportivo to find Villa Donato's large iron gate in a welcome position. After a brief rundown, Bill handed over a small plastic hand rake and the official olive picking gloves. The gloves were waterproof and covered with small white nubs. I'd never seen or worn anything like this before. Straddling the tree trunk and the top of the ladder, I was the one dedicated to the highest branches, which happen to be where the fruit is most plentiful. Unlike its tree relatives, these drop few leaves in autumn. Specific technique is in order when gathering all the fruit to one end of the net which needs to be poured into the waiting plastic cassettes. Just one dump on the ground imparted a lesson I wasn't happy to repeat.

As the sun moved behind the hill and our stomachs longed for La Tufa, our very favorite pizzeria, Tina declared our work for the day was complete. Carefully loading and stacking our take into the one-car garage, the prediction was made that just half of Sunday was needed to finish our Italian, British, and American Olive Harvest.

Sunday afternoon, with the rest of the olives picked and all 125 pounds of our bounty jammed into the back of Bill and Tina's green Fiat Punto, our caravan met at the *Frantoio Riuniti* on the other side of Cortona. Being the first farmers of the year, we found the oil press quiet except for the owner. Little did I know this would be a reunion. The owner was the same 70-something Cortonese that hosted a field trip we took while in my six-week language school a few years back. His rate of speech was still the 100 miles an hour I remembered from before. Thanks to the bit of Larriano I had developed in the interval, this time I was able to stay with him.

Pouring our lot into the water, I took notice the leaves and sticks stayed afloat while the olives remained a bit submerged. The pool gave way to a giant stainless steel dish. Rolling with the assistance of a hydraulic arm, a pair of four-foot stone wheels on end rolled and crushed our bounty into a paste the consistency of oatmeal. The mush found its way down a narrow channel and onto 1-inch-thick round mats being stacked five feet high. At the desired height a very old, red, hand-truck-like device placed the stack of mats under an industrial press. With water running from above, the wicker let go a murky liquid that ran into a centrifuge. Within moments a bright, thick, very pungent lime green liquid began filling Bill's 20-liter stainless steel silo while another waited its turn. Sixty-five trees had produced 37 liters of the world's finest unfiltered, first cold press extra virgin olive oil. I ran my finger across the final drop to steal a taste. A peppery but very smooth flavor filled my throat.

Back at Cà di Maestro, Piero soaked the end of a piece of bread with our gift from the earth. With index finger to the cheek, he made his approval purely understood. Nearly 60 days later, Signore Farsetti began dragging the nets and yellow plastic cassettes from the old shed. With temperatures half that of our first farming adventure, I found pace was the name of the game. With Piero's friend's Ape Motorcycle truck near, our freezing hands stacked the plastic containers as fast as they filled and we made our way to a different oil press. In a building at least 200 years old we waited with many others for our crop to be pressed. In the corner fireplace a metal grate was busy toasting bread. Piero wasted no time spreading his new oil and letting us be the judge. Thus began an affinity for only the best oil and a much deeper love of that tree that keeps my head from burning during the summer.

Val d'Orcia

Cà di Maestro on January 26th
❧ 2005 ❧

"It snowed, Larry, it snowed!" Jill's excited voice called from the kitchen.

We had a slight feeling it was coming as we returned from Rome by train 24 hours before. Everything from outside the Eternal City to just prior to our stop, Terontola, had been hit by the weatherman's correct forecast. As we approached Cà di Maestro our eyes could see that the same hills we'd been hiking just 30 days prior might now require equipment similar to that necessary for scaling a glacier.

We've become particularly fond of these hills, sometimes spending close to half a day wandering around 13th century borgos or taking a narrow dirt road just because it would take us higher than the main course.

We have found there is life in them there hills.

"Buon giorno," quipped the wiry seventy-something man, surprising us from behind as we paused, taking in the views of the valley below.

"Buon giorno, a bella vista," I replied, trying to say something simpatico. "Permesso a continua (can we continue)," I requested, noticing Jill and I could very well be walking right though someone's front yard .

⚘

"Sì sì, visitare mai?" He said inquiring if this was our first time up the hill.

"Sì, prima volta (our first time)." Extending my right hand, "Sono Larry e presenta Jill, noi americani."

The old man was Giuliano. Born in the large villa at the base of the hill, Giuliano has spent the better part of his life bringing this 700-year-old row of ten homes back to life. Without completely understanding his proposition, we spent the next hour walking through each of the four rustically restored buildings. He often stopped to make sure we understood each one of them was restored to its original condition, which was obvious to us, noticing the comforts of home then and now greatly differ. The further we progressed on this unscheduled tour the faster Giuliano spoke. Our comprehension fell further behind but we continued to reply "Sì, sì," with our heads bobbing like spring-headed toy dogs.

Once outside, Giuliano handed us a business card and explained that anytime we had friends needing *un posto tranquillo in affito* (quiet place to rent), we should contact him. He even made note of his e-mail address. As we continued up the trail I showed Jill that although he sticks to speaking his native tongue, his entire business card is printed in English.

Each day throughout spring, summer and fall another walk produced another unusual discovery, including one climb where we found three very friendly horses. On another, we ended up collecting several dogs that stayed with us for hours. When we returned to the car, all five *cani* seriously thought they would pile in and go along.

But now as the daily temperature rests near zero gradi, we've made more soup than walks. Potatoes, garlic, onions, celery leaf, brodo, pancetta, and just a hint of peperoncino enjoyed next to a blazing fire now keep our blood moving.

Shaking the red wine cobwebs, I reluctantly left the warmth of two down comforters to join a giddy Jill at the kitchen window. As is Italian style, the snow wasn't just a dusting but more like a thick fluffy blanket. Accompanying the beautiful white pillow blew a brisk north wind.

Donning our foul weather gear we entered the frozen wonderland and gingerly traversed each medieval stair. Our newly-decorated dirt road had yet to host any traffic. Perhaps the gradual rise had kept the Alfas from trying. We took caution hearing the spinning wheels of a four cylinder engine over the rise. An old Fiat Panda was giving it a go. Neighbor Giovanni was trying to push, but the real problem was behind the wheel: Mamma was trying horsepower as a means of traction. She also had the wheels pointed toward the ditch instead of the driveway.

"Turnata sinestra," I tried, using what I thought was the international charade of turning the steering wheel left.

"Jusato, troppi neve (I'm doing it correct, there's just too much snow)!" She shot back, wrapping the tachometer for another shot towards the ditch.

Finally, Giovanni convinced his 75-year-old mother to change her tack and amazingly, with a bit of persuasion, the 1975 Panda was free and clear.

Prior to this arctic day, we had never thought reaching the bright yellow post office a quarter mile down the hill was much of an accomplishment. On this day with drifts of three feet and a strong *vento* coming from Norway, we thought more than once about returning home *subito* (immediately). Jill made the case that she was born in Michigan and so we continued.

The road beyond our country post office is strange to us. Right in the middle of this agricultural zone and neighboring stone structures, the age of which is measured in centuries not decades, stand twenty new houses. Each of the two-story plaster and paint three bedroom casas comes complete with a small yard and metal swing set. The yellow Fiat school bus retrieves its young cargo at 8 AM and returns them to waiting moms or nonnas in the early afternoon. Italian children attend school Monday through Saturday, ending their academic day in time to join the rest of the family for *pranzo* (lunch).

Our winter wonderland walk past this oddly-situated street revealed that where there are no structures, there is a very cold wind. With visibility hampered by blowing snow, I tested Jill's resolve once more. Her piercing blue eyes, the only part of her face not covered by both a hood and tightly wrapped scarf, said *don't talk, just walk*. The newly tilled farmland, normally reserved for high quality Tuscan tobacco, was now thick with ice. I felt as if I was on a hike in Siberia. Jill was trying her best to mark this special outing shooting pictures with her handy Olympus. Fresh powdered snowdrifts against the stone wall was a sight new to us and worthy of several snaps. After another quarter of a mile, technology changed our course. The dependable pocket-sized digital that had logged some 2000 memories was frozen up. It was time to go home. Only a full-face motor cycle helmet would have cut the subzero wind now blasting straight into our red faces.

Once back at Cà di Maestro, we almost climbed inside the *camino* (fireplace) to thaw.

Valentino Rossi, Max Biaggi, Giancarlo Fisichella
❦ 2005 ❦

SP 416 is the Stato Provinciale two-lane road running through Montanare. A Right at the post office is our norm. On this crisp late-February morning, our destination takes us left.

One might have a hard time determining the very center of our frazione di Cortona. The entire village consists of the Poste Italiane, Vera's coffee bar, Il Mulino Locanda, Giuliano's Total gas station and the Campo Sportive, host of last summer's two week communist festival. A tour of "downtown" Montanare takes about 20 seconds, but for most natives the *giro* is more like 10. Ours is the last stretch of straight pavement before climbing nearly 2000 feet through a series of well-banked switchbacks. After careful research watching Formula One racing events, I've embraced the term "finding the line". Italian speed demons Giancarlo Fisichella, Valentino Rossi and Max Biaggi each make a living in search of this pavement paradise. Simply put, if you're in this groove, you have little need for brakes.

Our trusty 1993 Volkswagen Golf with its powerful 1600cc engine and tired Bridgestones has found the line on more than one occasion. These special moments are reserved for car and driver only. Jill's stomach isn't line-affectionate and she's sure our twelve-year-old VW isn't either.

Twisty turns give way to a gentle rise beyond the crest of Mt. Ginezzo. Rounding the last sweeping right turn, we see, sitting proudly on the hill to the left, the remains of the 13th-century Castle of Pierle. Said to be the birth place of Pope Leo the Great and host to Francesco de Medici, King Henry VII of Luxembourg, Pierle's 100 residents now appear to prefer a dressed down version of its previous noble lifestyle.

With our Dutch guest Susan riding shotgun, we climb the paved base hill and carefully pass through the tiny village. At several spots, the medieval village is barely wide enough for our white four-door. Pierle's deteriorated 700-year-old tower, meant to protect Cortona from the pesky Peruginos, is today covered in cascading ivy. At 11 AM, the quaint borgo is absolutely quiet with the exception of a curious great dane, a lightning quick grey cat and a man sitting next to an aged metal shack from which hangs a small, orange, Husqvarna chainsaw sign.

Today, Pierle is still accented by last week's three inch snowfall. This means we need to climb a bit further up the hill to provide Susan a good photo opportunity. Trading pavement for half-frozen mud, my goal is to get the car high enough above the village for one of those unforgettable Kodak moments. Just as Jill begins offering her feelings on the ice and mud combination, the car stalls. Thinking I have killed it with the incline, I turn the key and listen to the starter wind.

"Larry, are we out of gas?" Jill tries, in a very controlled manner, recognizing our guest's presence.

I begin to imagine three people frozen stiff above a rural Italian village beyond the middle of nowhere. I have to react and quick is the order of the moment. Basic German automobiles built in 1993 lack two features Americans cannot live without. Power steering and power brakes have been standard equipment on all American cars for as long as I've been driving. Using my entire upper body and the emergency brake, I coast us down to a safe resting spot. I try the key again. Nothing.

In just five minutes, winter has made its way inside our car. Almost simultaneously, Susan and I remember the man next to the old metal shack. My mission is clear. All my hope rests on Mr. Husqvarna.

This is my first visit to a rustic chainsaw-repair shack. For many years I ran a storefront business on a busy corridor. I still remember the countless times people would stagger in and hit me up for "some gas money". In the childhood game of tag, now I'm IT. In my best elementary school Italian, I attempt to explain that I am a *straniero* (foreigner), which was obvious considering my mastery of his language. I go on that my "macchina" was "senza benzina" and I have a problem.

"Certo," he politely replies, confirming I had a problem.

For some reason my mom's line about being up a river without a paddle was playing in my head. We both stood and just looked at each other. *What's next Batman*, I thought. *Per piacere* and *per favore* both mean please and my request for a bit of gas contained plenty of each. Once again the American vs. Italian stare down was on. I've never pushed a car two miles in zero degree weather. I was hoping that accomplishment could be reserved for another day.

"Va bene, prende la macchina (OK, go get the car)," he reluctantly declares.

I rush back up the slippery steep hill past San Biagio church to find Jill and Susan with low expectations and freezing cold bodies. We aren't exactly dressed for a picnic in Antarctica. Once again using all the muscles necessary to operate a Mack truck, my nearly numb hands push our German four speed backward and slightly uphill to get the nose pointing downhill. With my shoes half full of mud snow cone, we gently coast to the necessary 90 degree hairpin to within reach of my new best *amico*. Turning too hard means another problem gas will not solve. A miss will send us tumbling into a frozen olive grove.

The Holy Spirit successfully delivers us within 20 feet of our destination. It becomes evident that two young, nice-looking blond women have an effect on the old man's desire to offer me a hand. Salvatore energetically removes the gas cap and shoves in a rustic metal funnel. As the gas and the starter become one, I begin to acknowledge my future and this romantic relationship with Jill will remain intact. After a hundred grazies and a hug for Salvatore from both blonds, I do my best to conserve the two-thirds of a liter which Salvatore adamantly would not accept Euros for. Once topped up in Mercatale, our discussion all the way back is how in the world we can return this life-saving favor to the burly guy next to the shack.

In the following days, our oven grows busy and Salvatore is our first priority. Although he is nowhere to be seen when I return with our offering of thanks, I'm pretty sure those will be the first and last peanut butter cookies Mr. Husqvarna will ever enjoy.

Roma

Santi Cristoforo ed Emiliano in Montecchio

🌾 2014 🌾

I didn't take inventory of where I was standing until the 5:30 bells moved left to right in earnest. This daily mark, calling the faithful to their knees, caught me by splendid surprise. For the sake of sleep, church bells were throttled 20 years ago in my home town. I love them. This is not our first visit to the Tuscan-yellow country church. Surrounded by a dozen tall cypress, Santi Cristoforo is a religious spot we remember with sentimental fondness.

Ten years ago, just weeks after surrendering a year of our lives to Piero via a handshake house lease, he made an unbelievable invitation. Would we be guests at his son Gianfranco's June 20th wedding? Our limited vocabulary did include the word for we'd love to: *Volentieri*.

As is tradition, the groom's close friends and family assemble for the last hours of his single life. For the bride, this holds true as well. Our morning *festa* includes prosecco, fabulous pastries, sliced prosciutto, and one *brindisi* after another. Every car in the wedding party ties a six inch white ribbon atop the antenna. With best man at the wheel, the groom's car sets the pace. Franco's sporting passion is Formula One and it shows. I happen to be a fan as well. Jill wishes I'd like something requiring less adrenaline. Joining the other 100 well-dressed invitees in a nervous stance outside the 400-year-old church, we're not quite sure of how this will unfold. Piero is trying with purpose to explain the schedule of events and I nod, affirming what I think he might be saying.

Another set of rapid-moving, late-arriving cars enters the normal confusion that is Italian parking. All three photographers make good use of these group photo ops. In the crowd I spot Alessandra. She speaks a little English. I expect she can explain how we should behave. The crowd has turned its attention to a sound not familiar to me. The two-story, 15th-century place of worship is on a long sweeping corner with more cypress standing tall on the adjacent acreage. A steady clicking sound is coming from the right. Everyone but us knows what's coming. I move as close to the street as possible but still cannot make my way around the sea of Italiani in front of me. As the head of a white stallion comes into frame, the sound finally makes perfect sense.

Margarita's cream wedding dress lies partly covering the lap of her father. The bearded carriage driver draws the reins and the crowd shows its enthusiasm as Franco takes Margarita's hand. My glance to Jill is one of wonder. The crowd divides to let just the bride and groom enter. This private time is reserved for prayer with the waiting priest. Santi Cristoforo ed Emiliano was not built to accommodate 200 guests. Chivalry has us under-40's standing for the 90-minute mass.

An Italian Catholic mass features many formalities I've not witnessed before. Signing the wedding documents is shared by mother and father, brothers, and sisters. The audience leaves the church before the bride and groom, for the priest is to have the final word with them. Every waiting fan that will take one is handed a triangle-shaped white cone with blue, pink, and white rice. Franco and Margarita are showered as the bells ring out.

Visiting Chiesa Montecchio, as most know it, feels, now, like the other half of the circle begun that beautiful wedding day ten years earlier. Hanging across the rectory door today is a large set of pink, blue, and white letters announcing *Buon Compleanno*. Elisabetta, the birthday girl, born to Franco and Margarita six months before we welcomed Daniela, runs to meet us. She is thin as a rail, with long chestnut hair and a huge smile. Elisabetta and Danielina, as they call her, have something special. Daniela is most excited about this day on our mid-July itinerary. With few common words it's been a fun game of little girl charades since even before they could walk. Elisabetta's parents, welcoming strangers to us on their wedding day 10 years prior, are now dear friends and each visit seems to bring more meaning between our two first-graders. My future tells me these two will be exploring each other's terra firma before I know it.

Ultima Avventura

✿ 2005 ✿

"Alle ore dieci questa domenica mattina, va bene," Piero said slowly making sure I understood he and Amedeo would be at our door this Sunday morning at 10 AM.

"Capito," I confirmed, feeling both joy and sadness of this forthcoming event. After one year living as italiani, this was to be our final *pranzo insieme* (lunch together) at Cà di Maestro. Our home-bound Delta flight taking us back to Seattle was just five days away.

"Ma, tornerete qui (But you're coming back)," has become a familiar refrain we hear when we tell people our impending travel plans. Not having yet made the long journey to America, Amedeo has suggested we come "solo per fine settimana (just for the weekend)." Like most of the other conversations we've had involving numbers, I find the familiar dull pencil and paper. Once I add up the three hours to Amsterdam and the eleven hours after that to Seattle, a deeper sadness sets in. We both realize our unforgettable time together is drawing to a close. Our mutual admiration is like no other. He loves all things American and I have a deep affinity for everything his birthplace gives me. He believes Tuscany is the best of Italy and I wouldn't disagree. Even though we can't use the precise words, ours is a unique and memorable brotherhood.

"Permesso," follows a rap on our half-opened paned front door.

"Prego, Prego," I welcome Rosy and Piero arriving with literally armloads of delicacies for our Sunday lunch.

"Quindici posti oggi per pranzo," Piero advises me with his customary warm and simpatico smile. Like a first grader I still have to quickly run the Italian numbers in my head before I understand. My brain's result: We're having fifteen for lunch in our 600-square-foot, one-bedroom appartamento! "Due tavoli ferri sotto, anche questa, non ć è un problema."

"OK," I say, trying to imagine our expandable dining room table, plus two patio tables from downstairs all arranged in an area no more than 200 feet square. One of the great facets of Italian culture is they need far less personal space than we modest Americans. Although reserved at first, Jill and I have come to love the lack of physical separation Italians need, especially after they've become *amici*.

Facing Piero, I quickly open and close my right hand three times making sure I understand *quindici* as fifteen. He affirms with a quick nod. Amedeo quickly tells me that during the two year restoration of Cà di Maestro as many as twenty hungry mouths sat in today's lunch spot. Adding new life to 400-year-old structures like Cà di Maestro is an attractive retirement investment for Italians. Also, as Americans, Brits and Aussies have bought their own pieces of la dolce vita, real estate prices have doubled in five years. Just twenty years ago Tuscan farm houses stood abandoned by the dozen. Fortunate for Piero, both son Franco and brother-in-law Sergio are *geometra* or general contractors. Each specializes in restructuring old and tired properties. I've watched with amazement as a house went up on the adjacent lot. It appears those who built America's Fort Knox must have trained in Montanare. Stack terra cotta blocks, add cement, face with four-inch-thick stones and don't forget the eight-inch-square decorative concrete headers for the windows. Options for a terra cotta tile roof are one, two or three centuries. We celebrated when the exterior walls were finished. On countless mornings beginning around 6 AM, the two builders broke rocks with sledge hammers below our bedroom window.

New spaces or old, one thing holds true: Italians long to fill them with family, friends and food. "Pui Sale," Amedeo says, handing me a steaming tablespoon of his just-created puttanesca sauce.

Cortona

Open Hearts
❧ 2012 ❧

Neighbor Primo stopped me on the dirt road last night. Or should I say the dirt road stopped him from proceeding? Cà di Maestro is half a mile up a dirt and gravel single-lane drive, off of which several families live. I'm amazed how fate often puts us and an oncoming car on the same path. I'm not sure how we decide who backs up to the nearest wide spot but we seem to do this dance a few times a day. After four days of lashing rain Via Vallecchia (as it's called) is showing its ruts. Daniela knows this road by heart. She knows Alfanso lives in the *Casa Grande Palazzo* behind the six-foot stone wall; she knows Giovanni's house is the one with the chickens running free; and finally she knows Primo and Francesca's house as her personal Disneyland in Italy complete with three dogs, a pony, and several hundred toys grandson Tommaso used to enjoy. You might say it's just generally the most attractive place she's ever explored. It's also part farm after all, so Jill is a bit leery of the table that hosts the rabbit, chicken, or turkey cleaning.

If you visited us today you'd immediately notice the remnants of a large party Piero threw for his great niece on Saturday night. The two white (20'x20') tents held 55 guests, two twenty-foot tables full of every delicacy available around here and a whole, spit-roasted (stuffed) pig. Piero took great pride as the pig carver.

Great niece Rebecca was showered with special gifts from well-dressed attendees all arriving well after the pre-determined start time of 5 PM, a very normal and accepted practice.

Just two hours before the party was to start I took a quick trip to the train station in Terontola, a 10-minute drive from Montanare. Jill and I were excited to welcome the Bernie family from Dublin. I stood on the *binario* (the train platform) with anticipation as this trip is a milestone for Joe's recovery from three back surgeries. The super-long train from Rome (bound for Florence) screeched to a halt. It normally waits about three minutes to load/unload. I heard the rail attendant blow the whistle which means the train is moving on, but no Bernie family. Inez, Peg, and Joe (daughter, mom, and dad) couldn't get the door to open to exit their train car. Inez was able to get to another exit door and open it, and just in time as the 10-second countdown was on.

Although they didn't let it show, I can only imagine it felt a bit strange walking into a party in a place you've never been, with people you've never met, and in a village where no one speaks English! Piero welcomed them as he does everyone with his congenial smile and plenty of comforting gestures. The party went off without a hitch even though Mother Nature sent driving rain with severe thunder and lightning. When it was time for all to go we used picnic table umbrellas to get everyone to their cars because anything else would have been destroyed. Because the aforementioned one-lane strada was awash in floating pebbles, each Audi, Alfa, Fiat, and Smart Car motored *senza tanta velocità* (without much speed), an activity difficult for both Italians and those, like us, who wish we were.

When we encounter each other on the gravel lane, Primo and I normally just wave or say a quick *ciao* if the windows are down. Last night, though, he took a hard stare at our grey nine-passenger Fiat Ducato, an unknown vehicle on this skinny road he and his nine generations before him have traveled. When he realized it was me driving, his wife (and Super Woman in our eyes), Francesca, yelled "stop!" They were just returning from the annual *Ferie* (all city market) in Camucia, the village just below Cortona. Twice a year this town gives everyone the day off and hosts a massive seven-block open market complete with fruits, vegetables, seafood, household supplies, clothing, toys, tools, candy, dry goods, live chickens and rabbits, and just about everything else that can be stored in an oversized van. It appears the reason everyone gets the day off is it would be impossible to get to your office even if you wanted to. Francesca appeared from the far side of the car with something she knew Daniela would love: her very own kid-sized Batman umbrella! Daniela had been at their house earlier in the week and wouldn't leave the stash of umbrellas alone. Francesca was proud to tell us Primo had picked it out. Daniela and Primo seem to have a special bond and he's the first to yell *"Danielina!"* when we arrive back home each time. Primo is never without a big project. Yesterday I heard the cement mixer going just after 7 AM. This was the day Primo decided he was going to terrace the yard of son Maurizio's house and install four stone steps.

"Aiuto, Primo (need help)?" I asked.

"No, meno progetto (a little job)."

I looked over a bit later and noticed the stones he was using for steps were three feet long and at least 150 lbs each!

Joe, Peg and Inez have been bitten by the Tuscan bug. Although Inez has visited Montanare twice previously, she's now realized just how much she loves this place. Her professional life in Dublin has her constantly on the move, often on an airplane headed to some faraway place. We're lucky because we get to see her about six times a year in Seattle. Joe and I have had several terrific experiences during their last five days here. Prior to retirement some 10 years back, Joe (or Pepe as we now call him) taught an apprentice course in a Dublin trade school. He also was part of an international competition that sought the best student tradesman in the world. Included in the global event was design and fabrication of iron. I thought he would love to have a look at the local *fabbro* (iron fabricator). He was in awe looking at tools and sharing stories (without words, just gestures) with the fourth-generation fabbro in Ossaia, the next village west of Montanare. I too, was amazed to see the fabbro working on a sea-themed gate made completely by hand from a design pencil-drawn on a large random piece of trash paper. Joe had many questions for the fabbro, but most of the words were way outside of my conversational Italian. So, when all else fails, gesture!

The Irish, American, Italian dinner table traveled to Franco and Margarita's house night before last. Franco, Piero's son, lives in Montecchio, another small village just 20 minutes west of us. Elena, Margarita's mom, made a fabulous dinner of penne with oca (goose) ragu, roasted rabbit, and, for Jill, chicken, all finished in fennel, garlic, and rosemary. I lost count of the bottles of Chianti but I'm thinking the load to the recycling bin will take both arms! Franco and Margarita's daughter Elisabetta (or Bette) and Daniela played nonstop for three hours. After we devoured the final course (vin santo and biscotti) Joe stood and thanked everyone while I tried to translate to Italian from his thick Gaelic-accented Irish English. Joe and family truly appreciate the Italians' way of living. Like the Irish, Italians gather and, in most cases, around a large table with lots of food and drink. It was as if Joe was right at home in Montecchio and he told them so. The evening ended with dancing to Dan

Zanes. Daniela led a group of Irish, Italians, and her own parents to "All around the Kitchen". Not to be outdone by a three year old, Margarita played the Italian version of YMCA, a very fast-paced set of commands that includes the gestures for swimming, hitchhiking, being macho, waving, and several others.

Jill and I are just amazed at life here because it's really not about the words as much as it is about taking a chance, sharing, and being open to new experiences without even thinking about it.

Montanare

Vicini in Montanare
❧ 2006 ❧

"Bentornati a casa Lorenzo e Giuliana, e Bellissima Daniela" shouts the large, pink, handmade sign. Once again Rosy and Amedeo have welcomed us like never before. Streamers, balloons, a generous chunk of parmigiano and a bottle of Brunello. We feel the love from our *cari amici Italiani*. It's hard to imagine where the eighteen months have gone since we last danced with this part of our souls.

Our maximum-weight baggage stuffed with *articoli infante* tells us we've been busy adding the next generation who will hopefully one day feel what we did as we passed the black and white Montanare road sign. It was as if we were going back to drive the streets leading to our first day at Italian school. Our rented silver Ford compact wagon purposely passed the miniature yellow Poste Italia the first time where the narrow dirt road ascends to Cà di Maestro. Jill points out Giuliano's nicely dressed wife as we pass the sole gas station in Montanare. The empty, one-room 1639 church hasn't taken in residents, and still fuels my fantasia of remodeling it into a perfect little country house.

Small doesn't adequately describe the size of this frazione di Cortona. Most mapmakers missed this piccolo spot nestled at the end of the Val di Chiana in eastern Tuscany. Most of the 150 Montanarese have known no other residence. Almost everyone spends at least part of each day tending the rich soil of Tuscan tobacco, tomatoes in every size and shape, corn for the *animali*, multiple colors of peppers. Sunflowers stand above everything else like abiding soldiers.

A single-lane gravel road leads to Cà di Maestro. The location of each ten-foot-wide pothole remains the same. Andrea and his wife still occupy the green bench behind the post office. The chickens still maintain a *casa rustica*. Something tells me these might be the distant cousins of those we greeted previously. The 16-room, Medici-era Palazzo, where the professor from Bologna resides, still stands proudly behind a six-foot stone wall. I've spent too much time imagining my life on this fabulous, private estate sporting the Nobile Florentine coat of arms. As Via Vallecchia rises, Giovanni's house is the same, minus the vineyard, which seems unusual as this was the spot mother goose would escape the Tuscan heat. On more than one occasion, we stopped to have a little goose dialog. Jill is sure this had a detrimental impact on them. On this late fall day the whole flock is missing. My experience says they'd reached the cycle in their goose life which requires a freezer.

Famiglia Burroni lives in the sunflower-yellow two-story opposite Cà di Maestro. Primo and Francesca are as excited to see us as we are to see them. Francesca embraces Daniela and the circle of our return feels complete. Primo, a nickname awarded the first born male is a compact, mid-sixties, stocky *contadino*, with pronounced features. He's often in the middle of another major project. Since we met nearly two years back, he's almost single-handedly built son Fabrizio a four bedroom house behind Cà di Maestro, constructed a seven-foot rock wall sixty feet in length, built grandson Tommaso his own play park, and put up a four-stall garage wedged into the hillside. His crew of three Albanians obeys his every command without further discussion. Francesca assumes all things domestic and then some. Jill is always impressed that no matter what the task, Francesca wears a skirt or dress, even if she's tending the garden, hanging laundry, selecting the lucky rabbit for dinner, or sitting on the veranda shucking peas. We find it equally amazing that four generations live beneath one roof. Perhaps a thing of the past in America, we know for sure this arrangement would not fly in our native land.

Mappamondo, or world map, is the name of our second-floor unit at Cà di Maestro. Having spent nearly a year here on our last visit, this feels like home to us. Daniela is immediately mesmerized by the open-beam-and-terra-cotta ceilings. I guess if you spent the first 10 months of your life staring at flat white surfaces, this really would be interesting. My first challenge is blocking the steep stone stair case and making sure we have no unwanted roommates of the six-legged, eight-legged or legless-and-scaled variety, all of which are possible. Proprietor, Piero, and wife, Luisa, always leave the place spick and span but occasionally a black scorpion wants to share the house.

Camucia

First They Talk

Italy is the one European country that benefits from alpine mountains in the north and a massive island in the south. The bounty Mother Earth affords means no one ever longs for something fresh on the kitchen table. In Montanare, with just 150 inhabitants, most take advantage of the rich soil to raise their own beautiful lettuces, tomatoes, beans, garlic, carrots, and cucumbers.

What they cannot grow themselves comes to them. While the Tuscan sun beats down in early summer, the *sole Siciliano* has, by then, finished its first season. Mere days after the southern harvest, a morning truck slowly climbs Montanare's one-lane road. Over a muffled speaker, the driver's raspy voice announces the opportunity to buy out-of-season gems like delicious watermelon, roma tomatoes, and beautiful tropea onions. We cannot resist. If for no other reason than to take another interesting photograph, Jill and I almost run to Francesca's driveway to meet the aged white truck.

Bread, too, arrives in this picturesque way. Giovanni's little white van visits Montanare at 10 AM every Tuesday, Thursday, and Saturday morning. His custom, clown-car horn notifies everyone on Via Vallecchia of his arrival. Making a quick spin around in Francesca's driveway he opens both back doors and the aroma is intoxicating.

The 20-something Giovanni is a *paneio*. He and his family bake 10 different kinds of Italian bread during the night in Sinalunga, a neighboring medieval village of 2000 people. Beyond providing incredible, delicious, just-baked bread, Giovanni is continuing a tradition of Italian life that dates back beyond the combustible engine.

He arrives and brings the community together. They come to buy his bread, but in keeping with Italian social customs, first they talk. All must share an opinion on either the latest soccer news or some political scandal. There is no hurry. The talk ebbs and flows and runs its course.

Primo, Piero, Francesca, and the few others then motion to their preferences. Like at the fruit and vegetable markets, no one touches the product except the proprietor.

Piero and Luisa occupy this fabulous spot 120 days each year, while foreigners like us seek a pause living la dolce vita. Our words sound different but our hearts understand both languages. Piero is the catalyst for settling into my adopted Italian soul. Although he works tirelessly to keep Cà di Maestro looking like a *Town & Country Magazine* shoot, the stout mid-sixties Cortonese demonstrates what is so appealing of Italian life. Lunches never end short of two hours and always include plenty of Chianti. I find it impossible to refuse another slice of just-carved prosciutto, fresh *melone* from Sicily, or Pecorino from neighboring Pienza.

Never does a mid-day gathering end without at least 30 minutes of shut-eye in a lawn chair beneath one of the dozen cypresses.

Montalcino

La Storia di Lorenzo
❦ 2008 ❦

*A*micizia is the Italian word for friendship. It's a word reserved for the special bond we're fortunate to share with a handful of families here in Italy. And although we love all the external things about Italy, it's the joy we experience around these friends that ties us to this place and it rarely includes any English words.

Before we arrived in Italy this year, our nearly-new Airbus A-330 touched down in Munich, about 750 km (500 miles) north of Montanare. There, waiting with great anticipation (for Daniela of course) were Jim and Susan, our friends and two former co-workers of Jill's. They, too, have fallen in love with life as Europeans. They prefer the German flavor and even after Jim decided it was time to say good-bye to his day job, the two of them could not imagine living a lifestyle that put job ahead of life. They're also sold on life with two wheels that pedal and daily shopping at open markets. Both have continued the study of German and Jim has become part of a regional acting troupe. They too are *amici cari*, dear friends.

Our initial mission when we arrived in Germany was to retrieve our Opel Astra station wagon, get to Jim and Susan's fabulous central-Munich apartment and take a well-needed nap. Our total sleep on the plane amounted to a 15-minute snooze.

With gray matter only partially functional, we made a walk to the large park and *biergarten* for the obligatory beer and giant pretzel while Daniela played on the scary (for mom) large play structure. The next day and a half was spent walking the markets, visiting Starbucks (excellent coffee), and looking for the perfect outfit for Oktoberfest which is in our plan book when we return here prior to the flight home at the end of September.

Our original plan called for pulling out of Munich around 9 AM. It was high noon by the time we actually hit the road for what should have been a four hour trip to Lake Garda, Italy's largest lake, just above Verona. What we didn't know was this was the final vacation week for Germans and Austrians before school begins in mid September. It took nine hours, the last two hours of which was less than 10 miles an hour because of traffic! Thank God for the portable DVD player and *Dora the Explorer* keeping three-year-old Daniela amused between naps.

Lake Garda is a picturesque body of glacier water surrounded by a dozen lakeside villages including Malcesine, home of our apartment for two nights. We made the quick ferry ride across the lake for a look at the village of Limone and made our way around the old town, a place ripe for great pictures. Daniela absolutely loved the boat ride and it was a refreshing break from the 90-degree heat.

We traveled south along the lake shore on our way to Tuscany with two stops in our plan book. Cremona is an Italian village with a very important past. This is the home of the Stradivari family of violin fame. It was in Cremona that the medieval fiddle was perfected into today's classical string instrument. A *liuteria*, of which there are many in Cremona, is a shop which makes Cremonese violins and cellos. The workshop of Stradivari made 1100 violins during its time, just 700 exist today. Our stay in Cremona was brief as we were trying to beat the 6 PM Florence traffic, which was 150 km south and we'd made a promise to our awaiting italiani friends that we would be present for dinner around the customary 9 PM.

We passed our planned second stop of Parma, but promised a *giro* (tour around) on our return route. Driving in Italy is stressful even for this American fan of Formula One racing. If you cannot travel as the fastest car in the left lane (up to 100+ mph), you're relegated to the right lane with trucks and traffic merging like F18s off the flight deck of the Abe Lincoln. Being a lefty, my lane is an easy selection.

When we arrived last year, our very special friends Amedeo and Rosy tracked us down at the grocery store. This year Jill purposefully avoided responding to their texts until we'd jammed our already-full Opel with the goods needed to get us through our first week. Completely exhausted, I pulled our car in front of Ame and Rosy's house only to be greeted by Sergio, the next-door neighbor who was just sure I was ready to come in for a beer or two. Only because he could see the white lines in my eyes did he let me off the beer hook. Moments later Ame and Rosy arrived home and our Festa Italian 2008 began in earnest. We made the short drive to Cà di Maestro making note of many changes and improvements to the narrow road to Montanare. Cà di Maestro owner and very special friend, Piero, was awaiting our arrival. Although uncomfortable for some men, a gentle embrace and a kiss on each cheek seem natural with him. We're arriving two weeks earlier than our normal stay at Cà di Maestro, which means the other three living units are rented. This year it's an entire family of 10 from Munich. One of them happens to work for Starbucks, so we immediately have that in common. They are quite happy to find out we speak Italian so they can communicate with Piero through us.

Rosy and Ame began cooking our (and Daniela's) favorite, spaghetti carbonara. We're pretty sure Daniela thinks Amedeo's last name is Pasta. Within an hour, Marianna, Laura, and Luca (daughters and soon-to-be-son-in-law) arrived to join the party. We raised our glasses and sang Brindisino (a traditional toasting song). Ame's pasta was unforgettable, as was Rosy's bruschetta. For dolce (dessert) Rosy made a seasonal treat of peaches in red wine with vanilla and sugar added. Ame pointed out that the sugar increases the alcohol content in the wine, a fact of which my head had already become aware. Daniela led us in one dance of "All around the Kitchen" from the Dan Zanes DVD before she retired at 11 PM. We said ciao several times and all of us hit the hay.

We lay quite low the next day around the pool and became friends with our German neighbors. They too found this special spot and are doing everything they can to keep it a secret. We made an international pact (non-binding of course) that this place would stay just between us.

To make our arrival completely official we took an afternoon stroll through Cortona five miles up the road. This storied village of 1500 people dates back to the rise of the Etruscans and never seems to change. The big feature for Daniela is the play area at the big park which is dedicated (unusually so) to past French luminary François Mitterrand. Jill ducked into the internet store while Daniela and I visited the park.

Just prior to Jill meeting us at the park I began to taste (in my mind) a pizza from our very favorite Pizzeria, La Tufa. The first words from Jill's mouth: "You know what I was thinking?" Let me guess: La Tufa! There were hugs aplenty from second-generation owner Emmanuelle and staff Roberto, and Claudio. The pizza (and pasta) only gets better and everything we eat (here and abroad) seems to be judged against this La Tufa standard. As we caught up with Emmanuelle she told us of her daughter at college in Florence and how her house with three roommates was a complete *casino* (a mess).

During a nice long walk around the area this morning we stopped at Vera's one-room store, coffee shop, message center, lunch spot, and bar. For less than $2.00, we both enjoyed our first coffee Italiano. While I'm writing, Piero stops by to make sure all is "tutti bene" or ok. He's handed me a white bucket which includes the following items he's just cut from the garden below: Fresh basil, vine ripened tomatoes, cucumbers, white onions, garlic, and of course scallions! I can't say "grazie" quite enough to the spirit that brought Piero and family to us. Lucky for us this is Piero's first year of retirement. For several decades he, wife Luisa, and family ran a busy gelateria in the nearby village of Camucia. I say lucky for us because every time he would come to Cà di Maestro he brought several containers of gelato and you have to eat it while it's fresh. No complaints here, larger pants come cheap in Italy.

One of our missions during this stay is to look at other possible places to recommend in this area. A palazzo on our dirt road walking route caught our interest a few years back. During an internet search, Jill found out this place had been turned into a residence for tourists. Like most places in rural Italy, there is no sign or obvious main entrance. After a walk around the large four-story, beautifully restored villa this morning, we encountered an elderly lady in her customary house dress. We asked if this was, in fact, a residence for tourists. She quickly answered that the person (Massimo) would be back soon. The word *soon* in Italian should be defined as somewhere between two hours and two weeks. Last September, prior to leaving Italy, I left a card on the door of Alfonso, whom we had met a couple weeks before our departure. Alfonso had his son Stefano send me an e-mail to say thanks for stopping by. That was in December! Although it is difficult to adjust our mental clocks to this pace, we like a clock that ticks only when it really wants to.

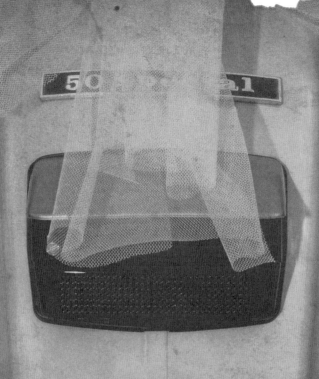

Pergo

Sorpresa Grande
🌾 2009 🌾

After a dozen-year courtship, Marianna and Luca have set a date. Ame and Rosetta's model-figured eldest daughter let us in on the June 1ˢᵗ wedding appointment as we began stuffing our oversized bags to return stateside. Sharing our disappointment that our frenetic use of the American time clock would exclude our attendance, we agreed our spirit would definitely be present.

Jill and I have admiration for these two young lovers. Having met in middle school, they represent a respectable tradition we've discovered amongst our circle italiano. Few unmarried Italian couples live together before tying the knot.

Following Ame and Rosy three miles out to Monsigliolo, we make a sharp right into a passage barely wide enough for our rental compact wagon. We slowly pass piles of rubble and concrete mixing machines, Ame's arm motions me to the right. We're parked in the middle of five, half-restructured Tuscan farm buildings. One will be Luca and Marianna's after they are married. As is normal between us, Ame rests his right arm on mine and uses the other to illustrate. He demonstrates where the courtyard gate to Luca and Marianna's place will swing. Our walk-through feels like a hardhat tour but in Italy, hard hats and safety equipment in general, are optional. Restructuring a 17th-century village into individual living units isn't an unusual development scheme here. Throughout the Val Di Chiana, abandoned smatterings of these stone-faced structures in varying states of disrepair are at nearly every other turn. General contractors—or *Geometras*—re-imagine what these former farm stables could look like hosting two-legged inhabitants. Jill and I have sat through plenty of Tuscan lunches while Luisa's brother Sergio (aka Superman) does his best to explain how he remade Cà di Maestro into its current beauty. Even Larriano, the official tongue of Montanare, has a hard time translating architectural terminology. One of the finish features Superman made a priority to point out are the small terra cotta mushrooms that adorn the Cà di Maestro chimney. This ode to Ame, regarded as the valley's expert on all things fungi, demonstrates the strong bond between them. Like Sergio, Piero and Luisa's son Gianfranco earned his Geometra license. They both manage multiple projects, most of which involve restructuring similar-age building remnants.

Climbing the unfinished stairs to the second floor of Mari and Luca's soon-to-be master suite, I'm told this project has been three years in the making with another six months ahead. My admiration for this early-30's couple grows again. By the time they actually sleep here as a married couple, their dream home will be four years in the making. Family and friends are making the finish work financially efficient for this two-bedroom, two-bathroom project. Gianfranco's wife Margarita heads the bathroom, kitchen, and outdoor furnishings distributor. Sergio's crew will handle the tile, electrical, and final plumbing as most homes are sold as shells minus the important details like stoves, toilets, and cabinets. Our limited exposure to the Italian building world has led me to believe most projects include this kind of family-and-friends collaboration. Rosy is outside trying to explain how the rectangular courtyard will host a small outdoor oven and room for six to dine *al fresco*. My imagination is strained by the pile of rubble at my feet which includes everything from crushed bricks to rocks and broken terra cotta tile. As we shimmy our Avis rental out to the road, I'm once again reminded how traditional life in Italia and our contemporary life in the free world contrast. Our independence is the draw for many but I'm in love with this version of delayed gratification.

Back in Seattle and a month and a half before Luca and Marianna made it official in Italy, Jill summoned me to our home office. With a skeptical excitement in her voice, she pointed at one of her oversized monitors. A Delta Airlines announcement was offering an unheard-of round trip price to Rome. The window to travel included Mari and Luca's wedding date.

"Should we do this Larry?"

I acknowledged two thoughts: Luca and Mari will only tie the knot once, and we'll never see this airfare again. But with a flight plan already on the calendar for September, was it financially responsible to visit Italy twice in 120 days? Very few things make it onto my splurge list. But this opportunity seemed to qualify; it was a chance to do something truly special.

After confirming our financial judgment—"We're really going to do this?" "Yes, we're really going to do this."—Jill made the reservations. But we hatched a plan that would make this an extra-special appearance. Only Piero would know of our arrival. It was he who needed to reserve a place at Cà di Maestro, our happy place in Tuscany. As the days closed in, our excitement grew. I'd made it crystal clear to Piero that our afternoon arrival in Montanare would be a *sorpresa grande* and he'd be the only one in the know.

Feeling like three secret agents, Jill, Daniela and I made our way through the familiar connection at Schiphol in Amsterdam. Even at just 5 years old, Daniela fully understood our mission. Hers is a special relationship with Marianna and Luca. Scanning family photos of Italy trips past, each annual collection includes a handful of shots with Daniela joyfully between them.

We rolled north from Fiumicino in the mid-morning Rome traffic. At the Castiglione del Lago exit, I began to worry we'd be busted until I realized no one had any idea what model of car Hertz had issued us a few hours earlier. Once again, I began feeling a bit like James Bond as we slowly climbed the one-lane gravel Via Vallecchia towards Cà di Maestro. As was normal, Primo was at the worn plastic table on the veranda. Wife Francesca was hanging the clothes in the mid-day Tuscan sun. As I made the left turn between the eight-foot iron gates, Piero stood and took notice of our unknown silver Opal wagon. Neither one of us could stop smiling when I greeted him with the customary kiss on each cheek. We both acknowledged this was not our customary arrival. In every year past Ame, Rosy, Piero, wife Luisa, and many others would be awaiting our reentry into this life we feel so incredibly grateful to be a part of.

Without us knowing, Piero and Francesca had put together a strategy that I couldn't deny. Before I'd even backed the car into our customary private spot to unload, Piero had the phone to his ear. His first sentence to Rosy was: "Three wedding packages from the U.S. have arrived at Cà di Maestro." He described them as *una piccola, una media,* and *una grande.* As good fortune shone upon us, Marianna and Rosy happened to be together and agreed to collect the packages right away. Francesca's plan included us hiding in Parco Tommaso, a term we coined for her grandson's play area in front of their large two-story Tuscan yellow house. Via Vallecchia, doesn't get a lot of action so most are vigilant of incoming vehicles. The anticipation was palpable. After two false alarms with us hunching behind a line of cypress trees, Marianna's Blue Fiat Panda came to a stop in front of Francesca's gate.

Piero directed Marianna and Rosy to collect the goods from Francesca who was waiting just inside her kitchen door. While their backs were turned to the trees, Daniela jumped out and said, "*CIAO!*" The screams could be heard in Rome, I'm sure.

My language set doesn't include much of what was said, but the tears coming from both Italian and American eyes marked this most incredible surprise. After everyone was able to breathe again, Rosy dialed husband—and my Italian best pal, Amedeo—to share the news. He said it was impossible that we could be in Montanare. Rosy handed me the phone and I assured Ame that we'd come to celebrate this most important family event. His long pause made me think our call had disconnected. When I realized his emotions had the best of him, I reacted with my own tears. Few friendships in my life have ever been more meaningful than this one. To think we don't even use the same words but today I'm more convinced than ever, love is a universal language that isn't made from consonants and vowels.

San Galgano

Amedeo Is Hurt
❦2008❦

I read the short email from his daughter 20 times.

With my limited Italiano, I was hoping I was confused about what I was reading. The five words I understood without needing an online translation were: *ospedale*, *grave*, Amedeo, and s*otto macchina*. Ame was in the hospital after being run over by a car and his condition was very bad.

I sat paralyzed with fear. The very man who has literally made me an Italian lies in a hospital 5000 miles away and all I can do is cry. It does me no good to call or even respond digitally in depth except to say how sad I am. Ame becomes breakfast and dinner conversation in our American kitchen. Laura starts sending daily updates. His right leg may need to be amputated to save the rest of his already medically fragile middle-aged body. I begin to ponder an impromptu airline flight across the Atlantic. Jill quickly adds logic by questioning how my presence there would make any difference standing bedside. Although I agree, I'm so in love with our friendship. We're a multi-national duo that has developed a heavily textured brotherhood on his soil.

My memory begins to flash with favorite moments including the first time he held Daniela when she was just eight months.

He was the first to emphatically declare it was his country's best food, wine, and olive oil that gave me and Jill our long-shot opportunity to become parents. As I continued to recount our most important experiences in Italy, Ame was the keystone. I found it hard to go five minutes without imagining what a giant part of this experience he represented. I began to think of how much of his kindred spirit lived in me and how that might change if his presence was lost. This was the time that lacking a common language was very challenging. I began composing questions in what I thought were the correct medical terminology only to receive Laura's responses that I couldn't comprehend. My questions turned into true-or-false inquiries. This worked.

Ame was going to live. His time in the Arezzo hospital would be months not weeks. A message accompanied by a photo explained that Ame's right leg would be in traction for at least 30 days. It was an 85-year-old man that ran over him twice. Fortunately, someone heard Ame screaming in the hospital parking lot after the old man drove away. If the accident had happened anywhere other than the hospital Ame surely would have died.

The photos started coming with updates. Although many of these progress reports didn't create much peace of mind, the photos of Ame going from the hospital bed to a chair and on to his rehab center did eliminate my worst fears. Eventually the elderly man—who lacked a driver's license—was questioned and through a series of tough decisions was not charged but was held responsible for Ame's gigantic medical toll. As with most Italian *burocrazia*, the process of Ame getting early retirement from his hospital logistics post would be monumental. After multiple trips to Rome to be in front of one of the only three magistrates in the whole country that hear similar pleas, his wish was granted.

Each time we visit the old country, Ame and I rack up more history. I think back to that dark day. It's a constant reminder of how distance and lack of a common language make this brotherhood exceptional. Life in Montanare without Ame would be an incomplete and much-less-delicious adventure. He's taught me how to use my heart to do the talking.

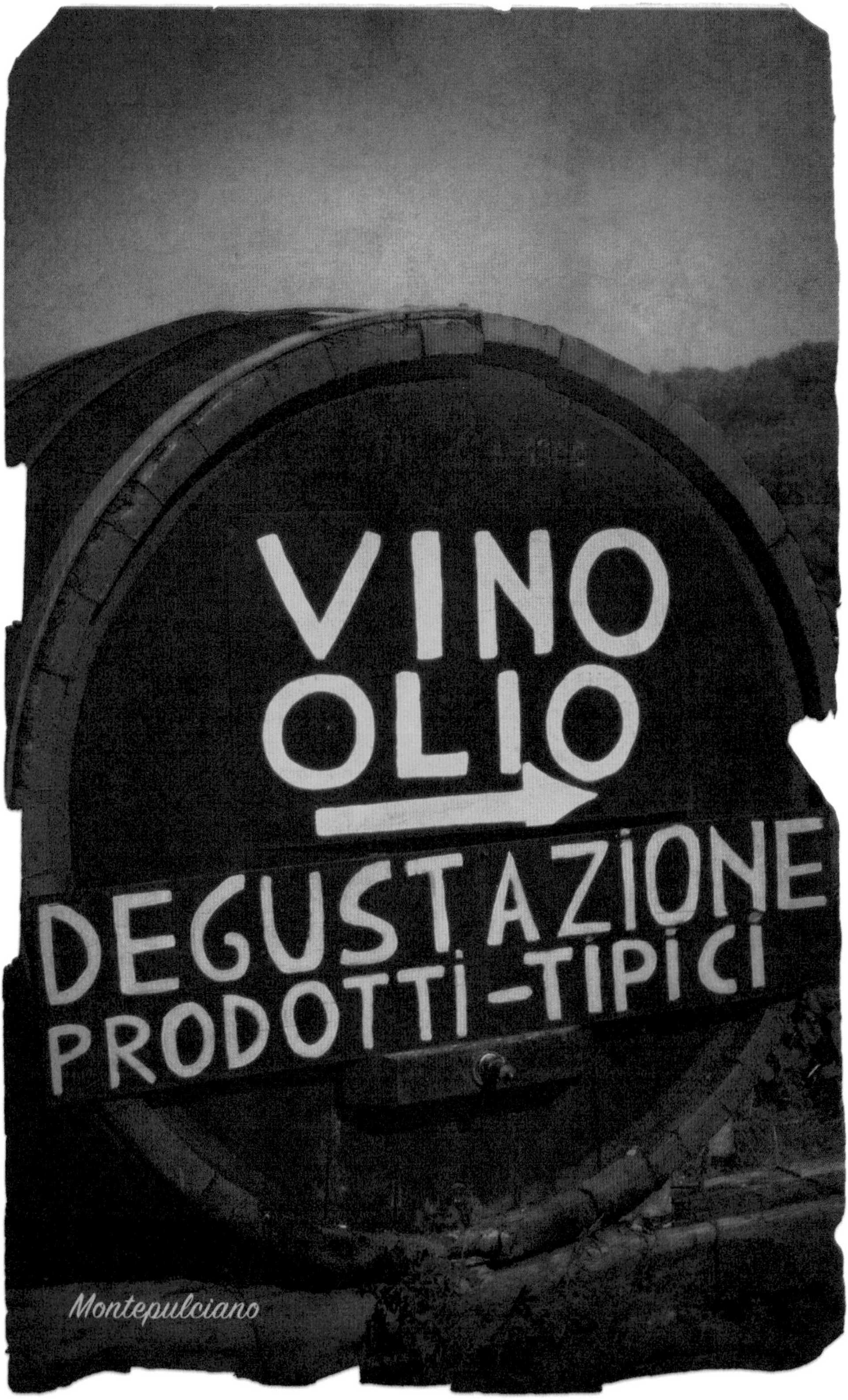

Montepulciano

The Pavarotti of Montepulciano

🌾 2013 🌾

Montepulciano restaurateur Pier knows what he's doing. He's been at this for most of his life. Based on the autographed photos of Sophia Loren, Robert Redford, among others covering the well-aged antique bar, I think perhaps his previous generations imparted this special skillset.

In a relaxed but mindful stance, the sixty-something, jovial, good-sized Tuscan makes it a point to welcome every guest as his first priority. It's not a hustle or aggressive move to make sure you're captured in his establishment, but one that feels like you've been asked over to share a well-cooked meal. While wife of 40 years, Elda, delivers her best from the kitchen, Pier makes good use of his public relations mission by first discovering everyone's native land.

Having chosen an outdoor table under a 15th-century arch and not far from Pier's front door post, I'm taken aback by how this silver-haired Italian can switch from basic Dutch to Tuscan Italian and on to Spanish in just one breath. All patrons receive this ambitious greeting even if they've paused just to study the menu. We've come upon Ristorante del Arci based on the recommendation of another shop owner in this magnificent hill town.

He assures us it's the only lunch spot that, in addition to its full menu, has the pizza oven hot. From previous experience, eight-year-old Daniela associates this central-Tuscan wine village with pizza. I assume these will be the things I'll look back on that were easy desires to satisfy.

Pier is taken by Daniela's thick blond ponytail and aquamarine blue eyes. Daniela's learned at an early age that Italy is a land of hands-on people. A slight index knuckle to the cheek and touch of the ear isn't odd to her.

"Bella Daniela," he quips after my introduction. This public display of affection by unknowns is common in Italy. I often find myself doing it to the little ones with no negative repercussions. Something tells me we've outdone the stranger danger message in the land of the free.

Pier greets a party of three Brit families and seats them behind us. Now the party really starts. Previous experiences have taught us that where there are Brits, Aussies and Dutch, a good time is imminent. Fortunately for us, Tuscany is a magnet for these nations to gather. Pier does his magic and within moments our table conversations merge. Like us, the Londoners are in love with most of central Italy and visit Montepulciano on every possible occasion. Outside Montepulciano's medieval wall, Range Rovers and Beemer's with right hand drive occupy several narrow parking spots. I'm still a little rattled when an oncoming Englishman passes me as if no one is in the driver's seat.

At some point in Pier's life, he developed a passion for emulating Caruso and Pavarotti. Once everyone is taking in their desired dish, Pier's musical offerings begin. He opens up, his rich voice filling the restaurant, somehow enhancing the authenticity of the rich Italian flavors we so gratefully enjoy. Pier chooses our guest and friend, Barbara, to receive his direct musical affection. Gently lifting her by the hand, he concludes his aria with a swoon that Barbara will be talking about for years. Although his audience of five tables wants an encore, Elda's voice from the *cucina* notifies him a hot pizza is waiting.

As in most establishments in Italy, one should never expect the check at Pier's before it's requested. Although this national tradition fits well on me, it's quite common for our dining experiences to stretch to four hours. While I stand behind Pier's bar so he and Elda can give me the family rundown, including his disappointment that not one of his three kids has an ounce of interest in adding another generation to the family, Jill and friends are standing near in the doorway with the "let's go" stare. I request *il conto*. I have great admiration for the accounting system of today's lunch for us five. A small tablet and a number two pencil total a random figure that must include the friends-and-family discount. I acknowledge my approval with a short stare into Pier's blue eyes and gladly lay down my Euros.

The Table

2012

Dread might be too strong a word for it, but I seriously dislike departing Cà di Maestro. At least 50% of my soul lives in this tiny Tuscan *paradiso*. Twenty-five out of 365 days is not enough, but it's all our frenetic American lifestyle will allow.

Piero and Ame have made it clear that tonight will be the biggest farewell ever. The outdoor tables await hungry friends. With 4th of July banners still hanging above us, Piero and I have counted several times to make sure our assembly of long tables can host a party of three dozen. Our spirit turns melancholy as we pause to revisit a few of our best times together. Piero's tanned face lights in a smile and he chuckles recalling the time Jill and I went wild planting 50 tomato plants. He's equally simpatico as he recounts some of the favorite guests we've brought in tow. In the past decade many have made the global crossing with us. Cà di Maestro is common ground among many of us. It's a rare occasion when there isn't at least one friend sitting at our American dining table who has visited our Italian oasis.

Francesca is crafting fresh focaccia and pizza in the wood-fired oven. Ame is creating our favorite buccatini amaticiana, a spicy pasta dish from the hills northeast of Rome. We attempt to recreate his signature pasta several times a year in our own cucina Americana. Although our stateside passion for buccatini is the same, rarely does our creation match Ame's artistry. I'm pretty sure I cook it more to visit my Montanare soul than to feed family and friends.

Tonight we are at the outdoor tables, though it is the table inside—the thick, walnut trestle table with six straight, high-back chairs—that is the center of our life at Cà di Maestro. At the walnut table, with mere inches between us, Ame often shares his disgust for Italian politics and with the next breath his unending loyalty to soccer club Fiorentina. His arm resting on mine, with a more serious tone, he often recounts family times with his late parents Bruna and Libero. To count the hours spent at this table would be impossible. I'm never ready to leave this table. It's hosted dozens of unforgettable five-hour dinners, card games that required our instruction, and birthday celebrations sung in two languages. Daniela, at just 8 months, fell in love with Ame and Rosy's spaghetti carbonara, her legs swinging from her chair mounted to this very table.

Today, the table is piled with the generosity of many. We've received parting gifts and have no clue how they'll make it home with our current luggage arrangement. Lucky for me, Jill is a master packer. She's also managed to accumulate enough miles to keep the airline weight police at bay. Even with her skill, Jill must find a way to include a double magnum of wine and its handmade wood box, given to us on the eve of our return trek around the world. After a brief analysis we realize the cellared wine is worth much more than the clothes we must eliminate to make room. Additionally, and as meaningful, artisan ceramic gifts also await a place in the bulging bags.

Outside, Piero's laughter and his stories trail off into silence. Together we cover the tables with white butcher paper and prepare for a final farewell.

Civita Di Bangoreggio

Doors, Shooting with Curiosity

⚜ 2014 ⚜

I go nowhere in Italy without my Nikon. The most important lesson for a photographer is similar to the Boy Scout Motto: always be prepared. Having a creative passion the life of which is far from home means nearly relearning the craft every 11 months. Photography and riding a bike are not even close. Digital technology changes and upgrades make a photographer's reasoning similar to that of a boat owner who always thinks the latest model is critical and the guy behind the counter at the camera shop knows it. "Why would you want that beat up 2-year-old camera body when you'll shoot incredible images with this shiny new model?" He's right, I convince myself. We travel halfway around the world, buy three plane tickets equaling two mortgage payments, rent a car for a month that requires 10-dollar-a-gallon diesel, and spend the whole time looking for the perfect Kodak moment. How could I not want the latest and greatest?

My lapse of decent logic got the best of me when I went looking for a new lens that would capture that impressive landscape I keep seeing near Montepulciano. It's that mid-morning shot where the cypress and what's left of the green fields nearly match. I've interrupted many a trip to Val d'Orcia to "take this quick shot"

☙

only to spend 20 minutes trying to get an angle that doesn't include the ugly power lines or wind-worn metal cabana. I know I have outlasted my companions' patience when the car horn sounds and I find myself in a wheat field 1 km away.

It would be impossible to deny wanting to get that same shot I keep seeing on the travel site enticing nomads to experience la dolce vita. An equal challenge for me is walking through just about any 17th-century Italian village. I cannot pass an interesting door or, for that matter, window, without making them my focal point. Each one is completely unequalled and nearly all are candidates for another look.

Part of me collects these images because I know my stock photography collection never seems to have an excess. The sentimental part of me shoots them for what they represent. Our experience has taught us that Italians are fiercely proud of their homes. Becoming a guest in them is a long-term proposition. Based on feedback from other Italophiles, the fact that we've been behind many of these entryways is culturally unusual. I'm not quite sure why, but Jill, Daniela and I have sat at many a *tavola Italiano*. Most of this good fortune is due to local introductions. Some is just plain luck and my lack of cultural awareness. Ame and Rosy have made us comfortable around their rectangular wood table on more occasions than I can count. When Mother Nature's plan is favorable a similar-shaped patio table serves as host on the giant veranda.

Ame takes his cooking as seriously as anyone I've ever met. With hand firmly planted on my forearm, he moves within six inches of my ear to explain the benefits of whipping the separated egg whites when making the perfect spaghetti carbonara. There is little chance I won't comprehend his instruction. Ame has had a hearing challenge for the entire decade we've known each other so his volume is sufficient to reach everyone in the room.

Although our mother tongue is different and he often must explain everything a minimum of three times, we share an important common life philosophy. I'm not sure where or how long ago, but one of life's lessons that came to me early is the rule that we should live, learn, and pass it on. Ame and I see it as our mission to get each other excited about the experiences we've had as a way to add value. Some current thinkers consider this social currency. I like to think of it as enlightenment for all that will listen.

Ame's passions have become mine through this method of continuing education. I think of it as another door he's held open for me, the one to his Italian soul. Since my first visit to Rome 20 years ago for a college summer abroad, I always wanted to be Italian. Ame has let it be so. Some doors are made of wood, others flesh and blood.

Montanare

Eating and Saying Ci Vediamo, Goodbye!

2008

Walking out to the storm-beaten, metal shed with a final load of Tuscan laundry, I picked up that scent that fills the air only on Sunday mornings. At first I thought someone was cooking breakfast but then my nose and brain remembered something much better. Neighbor Francesca rapped on our door last night around 10 PM asking us to Sunday lunch, a tradition among us. The mouthwatering smell wasn't breakfast at all. Francesca is rather famous (and not just with us) for Sunday meals cooked in her *forno al legna*, her outdoor oven powered by seasoned olive wood.

Francesca ran through the menu options last night. The following will appear, though not on Jill's plate: Wild Rabbit, Wild Boar, Lamb (neither wild nor unwild), *Figato* (liver), and even an animal Francesca's husband, Primo, says is similar to a deer. That leaves (for Jill) roasted chicken, along with Francesca's famous potatoes with fennel, garlic, black pepper, and a handful of salt. I think I've figured out why Italians don't have a sodium problem: everything gets washed down with red wine.

As she stood in our kitchen Francesca began explaining (with significant animation) the reasons why we should get together for our annual feast. Like many Italian super-moms that have done absolutely everything around the house, farm, and garden, Francesca is beginning to experience the vacant nest syndrome. I use that terminology with purpose as no one has actually left the nest, they've just re-prioritized how they spend their time and the dinner (or lunch) table has fallen down the list.

When Jill and I first found this slice of heaven in 2004, you could count on that familiar set of cars making its way up the drive at 12:45 for the customary two-and-a-half-hour lunch and *riposino* (nap). Sons, Riccardo and Maurizio, along with their wives, Chiara and Katia, also used to be absolutes for the 8:30 PM dinner every night. But, as Francesca explains, they work later and are too busy to come home for lunch. It's evident she misses life as it once was. She even stands waiting patiently for the odd-shaped yellow school bus that brings grandson Tommaso (age 6) home, even though his mom, Chiara, is right upstairs. Over the past couple years Primo's mother and Francesca's mother, both of whom once lived with them in the house, have taken their places in the cemetery, resting with many of their relatives. These trends of the shrinking family are not exclusive to the Burroni family. Italy is currently last in the birth rate contest among members of the European Union. The country is relying more and more on immigration to keep their weak economy going.

Those issues are not of concern here in Montanare though. Sunday in September here means it's *cinghiale* (wild boar) hunting season. On Sundays from 7 AM until 3 PM gun shots echo through the valley, one about every three minutes. The *cinghiale* is a rough cousin of the standard *maiale* (pig). Its wide snout has a small hook on each side. It is sought after in Italy for its terrific meat used in pasta sauce and for deli meats like prosciutto and salami. From what I can gather from Primo, getting a good shot at this animal is a bit like hooking the big one on the lake. If you catch three a season (September-January), you've done well.

There's a sadness among us right now. As we make our departure plans everyone keeps saying *prossimo anno* (next year)? Of course we respond positively but many things must fall into place each year for this trek to continue. There's also a real curiosity among our Italian friends about why we keep coming back to Italy. Cà di Maestro plays host to countless families during the summer months. Rarely (if ever) do any of those same guests return and we are the only Americans that have visited Montanare. We try to explain our love for many facets of their country. We also do our best to be sure they know their friendship is the reason we keep coming back to this specific spot in Italy. Most of the time my message gets through. I know this because the Italians (men and women) are not afraid to hug or lock arms to show their affection. Both Jill and I finally embraced (literally) the physical affection these special people show us. I'm not sure I would kiss a man on both cheeks in downtown Seattle, but in Italy it means we are close and plan to stay that way.

We made our way across the dirt road, which would have been easy to do even if we were blind like music icon Andrea Bocelli. I could have bottled and sold the smells coming from the *forno al legna*. Not only had Francesca roasted the aforementioned collection of two- and four-legged animals, but she'd also instructed Primo to barbecue several *bistecca* (steaks) as well.

Before we even sat down for the *Festa Domenica* (Sunday Feast), I was a bit concerned about a "light dinner" plan we had with Amedeo and Rosy. We didn't want to repeat an event from last year where we ate like there was no tomorrow, forgetting that the same-style event was to follow just hours later.

As we sat, Jill and I were reminded of something we learned while living here four years ago. Sundays are for family and nothing else gets in its way. No matter how busy you might be with other things, Sunday is Sunday. It's visible everywhere we go on Sundays. Grandmas and grandpas, moms and dads, aunts and uncles, and of course all the kids passionately kicking the ball around the yard as if their next assignment is a team on TV. Sunday is meant for gathering. You will find no businesses open on Sunday except a handful of foreign-owned markets, and even they only stay open until 1 PM.

The pasta dish is typically the *prima* (first) dish of an authentic Italian meal and Restaurant Francesca makes no exception. *Gnocchi* (miniature potato dumpling pasta) in a ragu made with *oca* (goose) and *passato* (tomato preserves) made its way around the table of 10. Francesca had boiled the goose halfway and finished it in the wood oven. "Good" or even "great" are not adequate words to describe this creation. The dishes of roasted animals came next and Jill made sure to identify which was chicken, as the cleavered animals had formed a small mountain on the oval tray. The prized Francesca potatoes—those Jill and I spend 11 months a year trying to recreate—always come with the meat. This Burroni family knows how much we love them and yield us much more than we can possibly consume.

Unlike most of the rest of the world, Italians eat the salad course last. We've been told it's all about helping digest this trainload of food we just gobbled down. Rarely is the salad any more than freshly cut lettuce, extra virgin olive oil, and, of course, salt.

It should go without mentioning that each course earned its own glass of estate-bottled sangiovese red wine, the grapes for which, this year, we will miss helping harvest and crush by just one week. Helping make wine with the community is one of the most memorable experiences we ever had in Italy. Primo and Francesca care for and maintain the 5-acre vineyard adjacent to their yellow two-story farmhouse, but the grapes—beyond the 1100 annual bottles-worth they crush for their annual consumption—they harvest and sell to a *Cantina Sociale* in Arezzo, 20 miles north of Montanare. Some 20% of the grapes belong to the white varietals and are crushed for that purpose. A portion of those grapes are hung in the attic for three months and later crushed for Vin Santo. This 90-day hanging creates a grape almost dripping in sugar that, when crushed and aged for two years, is best consumed in small doses with an almond biscotti as *dolci* (dessert).

While we strolled Perugia's Via Vannucci yesterday, we passed by Sandri Patisseria and picked up a *Dolce Serpentino* (Sweet Snake), an Umbrian delicacy that after eating is supposed to keep the bad guys away. This small, sweet cake in the shape of a little snake finds its folklore on the shores of Lake Trasimeno, Italy's third-largest lake, located just seven miles south of Montanare.

As the provincial capital of Umbria, Perugia holds the keys to many significant talismans in our Italian life. A medieval college hill town of 150,000 inhabitants, Perugia introduced us to Daniela Borghesi, who helped us obtain our official permission to gain residency and is the woman who would come to be our Daniela's namesake. On every possible occasion, we try to carve out one hour from the elder Daniela's impossible city administration schedule and sit the two Danielas over lunch. She is an amazing fair-skinned, light-haired, and well-dressed, middle aged, Italian woman. A segment of her role is interpreting for the Mayor as the city's delegation visits Perugia's half-dozen sister cities around the globe, my native Seattle included.

Our gratitude for her grew out of some keen hand holding during our first month when we were attempting to get an unintelligible pile of police registration documents in order. Hers was the name given to the miracle that is the apple of my soul-centered eye.

Looking at a map, Montanare is just steps from the border of Tuscany and Umbria. There seems to be an admiration by Umbrians of Tuscans and vice versa. Umbrians appear to be better in the woods (hunting the animals that are cured for expensive meats), whereas the Tuscans have the wine and tourism business wired. It's rare we hear the same sharp-edged banter between these regional neighbors that we experience about how those living in the north feel about their brethren to the south. Even Ame, who is a Tuscan beyond belief, will concede the olive oil in Umbria matches up to the highly celebrated (and expensive) First Cold Press Extra Virgin Olive Oil on his Etruscan dinner table.

As Francesca handed me a demitasse of piping hot Italian coffee, I realized I hadn't really stuck with the "pace yourself, Larry" thought I'd had as this lunch began. I was stuffed and at this time couldn't imagine eating another bit of food for at least 24 hours. I'm confident the second plate of gnocchi maxed out my hollow leg and how could I have passed on real Francesca-roasted potatoes. They loved the gift Jill had created. The oversized coffee cup with pictures of our time together last year was very much appreciated and even Super Woman Francesca shown a moist eye as she relived our unique friendship. Like Ame, Rosy, and Piero, the Burronis are the people Jill and I miss the most in our "off season". It's the respect Jill and I have for how hard they work each day. Even in retirement Primo jumps out of bed each day with the idea that on this day no job is too big.

We finally caught up with Ame and Rosy a bit before 7 PM. It was evident they had expected us earlier, perhaps remembering our final Sunday together one year ago when we explored a set of villages near Perugia. As advertised the light dinner was on track. When it comes to Italian cuisine the word "light" is open to interpretation. *Pici* (pronounced peechee) is a very thick spaghetti-like pasta and is quite filling. Our light dinner menu included *crostini* (small toasts with sausage and a melted creamed cheese), crostini with truffle paste, *Pici* in a thick passato, roasted chicken, salad, and our once-a-year indulgence: Rosy's one and only tiramisu. And, once again, each course was accompanied by plenty of fabulous Tuscan *vino rosso*. Rosy wouldn't be happy unless we finished the entire tiramisu (that's my story and I'm stickin' to it).

One look at the outside of Rosy and Ame's fridge provides proof there is love between us. There are more pictures of Daniela and other Seattle memorabilia than on our own fridge. Ame, Rosy, Marianna, Laura, Stefano, and Luca, really are our heart in Italy. Without words of a similar language these six have helped us realize that fun is spelled the same no matter what the colors on your flag. They love Daniela as if she was their own and sometimes when I see how well she receives them it appears the feelings are mutual. Like Francesca and Piero, these six have allowed us to experience the most authentic Italy.

Although I was finding it hard to move, we really needed to get back to Montanare so Jill could finish the rest of our very well-organized packing—six suitcases that can weigh no more than 50lbs each. We've really learned to dislike these uncomfortable moments when we have to say goodbye, well knowing it will be quite some time between our last *brindisi* and our next American BBQ at Cà di Maestro. Jill and I both know it's these times with just Ame and Rosy that we need more of and yet our time together, at least for this chapter of our history, has come to a finale. Ame and I both hesitate to make eye contact because each year *noi piangiamo* (we cry) and how could either one of us MEN do such a thing to the other? The girls, on the other hand, know mascara is cheap and the tears run without reservation. We hug and we hug again as Rosy insists on belting Daniela into our gray Avis Opel wagon. I check the rearview mirror and I see Ame: he just stands with his hands in his designer jean pockets as if to say *please come back, we've really just begun to know each other.*

Acknowledgments

As I reflect on the beginnings of this journey, it inspires me to recall the dozens that have made **Miracles In Montanare: Ten Years in Tuscany** a reality. Ironically, Ellen Hoffman, my college French teacher, is the one who started this fire. That first transatlantic Paris flight was greeted by Europe expert guide Alessandro whom I renamed Romeo for all the right reasons. As that initial tour entered Verona, it was he who gave me my first opportunity to be Italian. In less academic environs, I met Deborah and Rem who are responsible for my blind-date-birthday-party introduction to Jill. From that connection came a special friendship with Chef Roberto Russo, another man who allowed me permission to become a passionate Italian. Chef Roberto sharing his network of trusted locals was the key to how Montanare landed on our map. This miraculous village is made up of so many loving families, including the Farsetti, Busatti, Burroni, Bruschi, and Accioli clans, all of whom have made this experience incredibly deep and meaningful. The center to this collection is Francesco (Accioli) who came to Seattle for three months. His family insurance business led us to Rosy (and her husband, Amedeo) whom we now consider the closest of family members. Ame is the brother I never had and our time together is where some of my most treasured Italian memories where born. Jill and I feel incredibly fortunate to have met Brits Bill and Tina Bain who taught us how to live like Tuscans while maintaining our native soul. We're also deeply grateful to Daniela's namesake (Daniela Borghesi) for being a wonderful friend and administrator of our Seattle-Perugia Sister City relationship. We owe great thanks to passionate Sister City advocate Mike James for his expert assistance with translation in this body of work. I have special gratitude for our storytelling consultants Catherine Lenox and Mina Williams who have helped me be more creative in my writing. My biggest appreciation belongs to publisher Ethan Yarbrough and graphic artist Sonja Gerard. There are few words that can express my absolute thanks for your unending efforts to get this dream to its best form. You came into my world at exactly the right time. My heart in this book belongs to Jill and Daniela. Without you two, I would never have found these layers of my soul to share.